Hear My Voice:

My Life Unmasked

A Memoir

Also by Barbara Mould Young:

Journey Down Under: Six Word Stories/A Poetic Travelogue. 2019. Self-published. Limited. Contact author.

Pelicans' Choreography: Poetic adventure tales and three short stories. 2020. Self-published. KDP

The Interconnectedness of Story, Community, and Health. 2013. Master's Thesis. Self-published. KDP

The Tree Is Medicine: Infant Mortality at Cedar Bay. Copyright © 2016 Pisces Publications. KDP

Travels To Maya: 14 Days in the Yucatán. Copyright © 2013 Pisces Publications. KDP

Gift: Poetry from the Woods. 1998. Self-published. Limited. Contact author.

Opening Doors: Stories of Public Health Nursing. 1994. Edited: Zerwekh, Young, Primomo, and Deal. First and Second Volumes printed by the Washington State Department of Health.

Opening Doors: 100 Years of Public Health Nursing. 1994. Documentary Video. Executive Producer. Major Funding: Washington State Department of Health, Individual sponsors, and the Robert Wood Johnson Foundation. Distributed by the Washington State Public Health Association.

Hear My Voice:

My Life Unmasked

A Memoir

Barbara Mould Young

Hear My Voice: My Life Unmasked
A memoir
by Barbara Mould Young

Published by: StoryVoice International
                 Olympia, Washington
                 y2byoung@hotmail.com

Cover sketch: Barbara Joslin Packard, Olympia artist
Cover design: Suzanne Fair, Olympia Copy and Printing

ISBN: 978-0-9894430-5-0
Printed in the U.S.A.

To My Daughters

Do you open the door of your home to let in the sunshine? Are you respectful of those who dwell within? What is going on behind the doors as you retire for the night?

I.   I grew up in a middle-class neighborhood of Dayton, Ohio, walked a mile to school, wore galoshes in the rain and snow.

II.   I married my college sweetheart, served as a Peace Corps volunteer in Brazil, and reared two daughters.

III.   My second husband lived an alias of which I had no knowledge, and I gave birth to my third daughter.

IV.   Divorcing again, I fled to the Pacific Northwest. Native women taught me to weave baskets and to make masks to grieve and to tell my story.

This is my story. It is written to the best of my recollection. Some names have been changed.

I write to discover what I know.

Flannery O'Conner

A root of the sacred tree still exists. Nurture it. Allow it to leaf. Bloom and fill with singing birds. Even in sadness, hear the singing birds. Loss in death, but rebirth. The self begins with me to make the tree to bloom. Nourish the root. The heart in the root of our human beingness.[1]

Black Elk

---

[1] Niehardt, John G. *Black Elk Speaks.* State University of New York Press. www.sunnypress.edu.

Contents

Foreword

I WILL BE EIGHTY YEARS OLD on my next birthday. How did I get here so quickly? How much longer do I have to tell my story?

January Six will be an anniversary of the insurrection at the United States Capitol in belligerent disregard for the sanctity of our Democracy. The insurgents believed the words of the former President urging them to become violent. I want to shout to these folks: "You are misguided, misinformed. You are led by a false prophet. The man is a fake. Why is it you want him to be in charge? Why did you take the American flag as a rod to stab, break and kill Capitol Police? I cried when I saw the news footage of your crushing glass.

I remember. I was twelve years old, standing on the steps of the Capitol in a Girl Scout uniform with a full badge sash across my chest and a green cap on my head. I stood with Troop 343 and Congressman Paul Schenck, a Republican from Dayton, and a friend of my father's. How proud I was. I wanted to return to Washington D.C. as a congressperson. I was sure it would be the way to serve my country.

I have had eighty years of making mistakes, but my love of country is firm, grounded in a democratic goverment I honor and respect. I have run for public office and served government at all levels—city, county, state, and federal. What is it these insurgent citizens see in a man who betrays, lies, takes no account of his mistakes, or even thinks he has ever made a mistake? The former president has no grace to concede a loss as did Al Gore, for the sake of country unity. My eighty years must count for something.

I grew up in Ohio, a state that is considered a swing in politics. Television networks interview Democrats and Republicans. It is the state of history, second to Virginia in producing Presidents. It is the state of universities and colleges, established early in the Republic; a land of innovation as in inventor Charles "Boss" Kettering and the Wright Brothers; a state of industry, corn, and soybeans.

Six years after I stood on the Capitol steps as a proud Girl Scout, I went to The Ohio State University, studied nursing, married, served in Peace Corps, divorced, married again. In second marriage,. I invested fourteen years with a man who abused my daughters, lied about who he was, and lived an alias. Second husband had the same anti-social personality as the former President. I denied the evil in second husband and, like the citizens who stormed the Capitol, did not recognize the deceit, the lies, the dishonesty. After divorcing husband two, I fled Houston and put distance between us.

Upon retirement from teaching nursing mental health, I facilitated mask-making workshops to allow participants to tell their stories. During a workshop, I move into a level of consciousness beyond myself, as if a sacred space exists to give voice to truth. John Lewis encouraged us to speak to the truth and to get into "good trouble" if need be.

What happened to the proud Girl Scout? Why did I divorce my college sweetheart? Why did I live with a man who abused, lied, and betrayed my love? Was I the person I was born into being? Where was my voice? In cherished memory of my first husband, my late relatives, and my dear friends who have passed on, I move my fingers to the keyboard. Hear my voice unmasked.

I. Girl from Dayton

1942-1965

I WAS GROUNDED IN THE MIDWEST, born into a city neighborhood, baptized in the Presbyterian church, and attended public schools. My mother was a devoted homemaker; father worked for National Cash Register. I had an older sister and brother. Within this home, I grew.

1. On Location: Voice of a Birthing Infant

1942

SEVENTY-NINE YEARS AGO, my journey began. I made my entrance after a prolonged push, followed by a slippery slide, of which I had little control. The force made me do it. I had successfully transitioned from the cramped, fluid, weightlessness of the womb to a world of lights, voices, and gravity. Shocked by this release through the tight passage, I threw my arms back, expanded my chest, and sucked in air. Then I cried. It was all in the script according to the protocol of the universe. I was a newborn in an earthly atmosphere. To the delight of witnesses, I had arrived safely. From that moment, I was destined to be a swimmer, a traveler, and a storyteller.

Gravity. If I were not being held by my mother or dad or a caring relative, I would fall to the solid earth and be crumpled. That's how the magnetic force of gravity works. Aafter I learn to crawl, stand, and walk, I'll be able to show how gravity works. As I am learning about this new transition, I want to describe the space around me.

To my left, a proud father is looking at me with approval, wondering how I might grow up to one day care for him as he is now caring for me. Daddy is 53 years old and the father of three. My older sister, by five years, is already taking charge as the eldest kid. My brother, three years older than I am, wants to teach me how to box so that he will have a sparring partner. How do I know all of this? Because my senses are acute. I am the smartest I will ever be. I have millions of neurons in my brain, absorbing all that is new, waiting for instructions. Of course, I do not open my eyes so much as I'm still getting used to the light, but I hear and feel it all. And, I sleep a lot.

Below me, I see a soft, cuddly blanket and the eyes of my sister who has shocking red hair. Even though I do not distinguish color yet, hers is bright enough that I get the idea. She is squatting to meet eye contact, letting me know she is in charge. Around the blanket are my mother's embracing arms, giving me the security of physical boundaries, letting me know I will not be abandoned, nor will I fall.

Above me, there is a loving face eager to nurse me. Mother has always been interested in the family's growth and development, and my birth is no exception. She plans meals for the entire family, so we all get our vitamins and appropriate nutrition to support peak brain development. Mom came from the farm, so she knows about this nursing and feeding stuff. She cared for the pigs, horses, puppies, and kittens long before she had her own children to nurse and feed.

Between her chin and mine is her breast, full of milk, and when I cry with hunger, mother will offer her breast to satisfy. I am learning the art of latching on and sucking. It is natural, and my survival. Her milk is warm, soothing, thin, and has all the nutrients I need, plus the natural immunizations from the diseases so prevalent in the community. When I am nursing, mother talks to me about the world I have just entered, wanting me to be informed.

One week later. "These are war years," Mother explains to me while I am focused on the nipple. "That means butter, cream, and gas are rationed. Childhood infections like measles, whooping cough, typhoid, mumps, and rubella are prevalent, and breast milk will give you temporary immunity. I am happy you're nursing from the breast."

Wrapped around me is a soft cotton blanket. and on top, a handmade quilt by a great aunt who used scraps of house dresses and period fabric. "Snug as a bug in a rug," is what my sister says, and she knows. At five years, she's been around. The quilt means I am sleeping under history and carries karma of the ancestors, pioneers into the Ohio Territory. Mom has been working on the family genealogy with her cousin Edith McCutcheon. Her side came from Ireland and Germany, while daddy is from Scotland and England via Canada. Because I was born on St. Patrick's Day, it's okay to say that I am Irish. It fits with the Finney side of mother's family.

Location. Mother was born in Pike County, southern Ohio. Father came from Niagara Falls, New York, to enter a work-study program at the University of Cincinnati. My neighborhood is Riverdale, near to the field where the Wright Brothers tried out their flying machines. The field ran parallel to the commuter line, where trolley passengers could witness history taking place, but they paid little attention. My parents talk to me of history, and although I appear to be sleeping, my neurons receptors are absorbing the teachings.

The world outside. My parents are preparing to set out beans, carrots, tomatoes, and corn in a Victory Garden on a plot leased by the YMCA. Keeping Mom healthy and happy with fresh produce from the garden keeps her milk nutritionally strong and in steady supply.

Love. When I awake, I study my surroundings. I am warm, well-fed, and embraced. My brother and sister are curious as to how I fit in the new sibling count and urge me to grow. They want me to play, but they'll have to wait. Later, I will crawl, walk, run, travel, and build a lifetime of stories, but for now, I am content to be held close, to be snuggled, nursed, and admired. All the fuss will settle in time. For me right now, it is nurse, sleep, learn; nurse, sleep, and learn. The blankets are snug; mother's and daddy's arms are comforting. I nurse, sleep, pee and poop, nurse, and sleep. Sleeeeeeep.

2. Memories of a Backyard Paradise

1949

MY FIRST HOME was a cream-colored painted clapboard, No. 49, on Fernwood Avenue, a neighborhood where the houses were different in design, but otherwise indistinguishable in their uniformity of size and layout on the street. Three square concrete columns on the front porch supported the roof overhang, and three broad steps arose from the walk which came straight to the porch from the city sidewalk. Small grassy plots on either side of the walk gave up the entire yard to two magnificent sugar maples. In autumn, these trees were the most spectacular on the street. Brilliant shades of red, orange, and yellow leaves surrendered themselves to the building of leaf forts, and were raked into crunchy piles for jumping, or tossed in the air to again float their way to earth. Playmates and I inhaled the leaves' musty smells and tasted the season. Leaves' dying presence made us feel alive and we laughed with pleasure.

On the left lived the Hesselman's at No. 47. Twins Joan and Joyce were my sister's age. I often heard the twins calling across the space between houses, "Hey, come over to play with us, but don't bring your sister; she's too little."

In the house to the right, No. 51, across our gravel drive and low green hedge, lived a husband and wife my mother's age, and the wife's elderly mother. The three of them never smiled. Seemed as if they lived inside their house and only came out to reprimand us kids for some infraction. "Hey, don't step on the lawn." The sound of our voices brought them out of their house to guard the grass. Their lovely lawn remained untouched and un-played upon; no dirt spots worn through. A sad lawn it was, yearning to be loved.

The city sidewalk was trimmed by a six-inch-high curb. Sitting on the curb during a soft summer rain, I felt the water tumble over my bare feet on its journey to the Miami River. How happy I was, alone with the rain.

The front yard maple trees were not for climbing. The lowest branches, twice the height of my father, were out of reach. The trees were proud sentries, royal guards to the simple home they protected. But it was the backyard which was our playground. Three short concrete steps at the back stoop brought you from the kitchen door to ground level. My brother Jerry and I sat on the stoop to string green beans, which felt like velvet, freshly picked from the Victory Garden.

Near the fence line with the Hasselman's was a tall stately Golden Oak with branches low enough for the building of a tree house. My father, who studied civil engineering at the University of Cincinnati, and my brother Jerry planned to build the tree house. Within the bifurcation of the branches, a wood platform was constructed, complete with guard rails to enclose the platform. Seven 15-inch wood slats were nailed into the bark as steps. A strong rope was suspended from a branch above the platform that could be used not only to help the climber but also to assist in hauling a bucket to the platform.

One afternoon mother gave Jerry and me the task of stringing a large pot of green beans. When she was back in the kitchen and safely out of sight, we looked at each other in knowing conspiracy, and took the bean pot to the base of the tree. Jerry climbed first. We roped-in the pot, and he pulled it to the platform. I followed the pot. Our task was made easier as we had perspective of the world, the backyards of our neighbors. We were laughing at our inventiveness, having fun, until… Mother came to check on our progress.

"Jerry! Barbara! Where are you? Where are the beans?"

"Oh, hello, Mother! We 're up in the tree house!"

"You get down here this minute!"

Shocked that mother did not share our enthusiasm and perspective, the fun retreat ended abruptly. Jerry and I successfully lowered the pot to the ground without spilling a single bean.

3. Wringer Wash Tub, Dancing

OUR HOUSE RESTED UPON A STURDY, DEEP, CONCRETE BASEMENT. On the east and west sides, light came into the basement through ground-level windows. One could access the basement stairs from a landing, which had an outside door on the Hasselman side of the house. In the center of the basement stood a huge black furnace, with tentacles like an octopus reaching up to floor registers. carrying warmth to the entire house. To feed the furnace, coal was shoveled from the coal bin, my father's job.

In the basement, Mother washed our clothes in a wringer wash tub, which was connected by sturdy hoses to a heavy concrete utility sink. Staring into the washer, I watched the agitation, mesmerized by the dance taking place. Central Agitator was the lead partner. With a working hum as background music, Agitator swung the clothes first in one direction, as if in a waltz, and then, pausing to let the movement mellow, reversed the dance to go in the opposite direction, returning with a polka. Water accompanied the movements, like waves of the sea, a constant rhythm of in and out, back, and forth, squeezing here, rubbing there. It was a dance of contact and intimacy. When Agitator was spent, the dance slowed. She paused to allow water to be released, while expressing satisfaction for a dance well performed. Rushing to be free, the soiled water, with its claimed dirt and grime, pushed through the exit hose into the concrete sink to drain its way into the city sewer system, leaving the clothes limp in the tub. Next, they moved through the accordion jaws of the wringer which extracted remaining water. Clean and wet, the garments were removed to an oval reed basket and carried up to the landing and out the side door to the back yard for hanging.

A long clothesline extended from the corner of the garage to the edge of a small garden that extended from the back stoop. Onto this rope clothesline, Mother pinned the garments, grabbing the shoulder seam on shirts and pinning equally on each shoulder so that it hung in the same position as wearing it. Pants were hung from the waist band. Undergarments were hung open to the sun. When the laundry load was placed to her satisfaction, Mom propped up the line with eight-foot metal poles with hooks on the end that hoisted the line high into the air. The clothes seemed to enjoy hanging well above ground level, room enough to dance with sun rays and high enough to flap and fly as the breeze energy allowed. It was a happy childhood.

4. Playhouse and Entrepreneurial Start

MY FIRST PLAYHOUSE was built by my grandfather, James Rufus Finney. While he was one to give wise counsel to his friends on farm management, the law, and education, to me he was a skilled carpenter and my medical advisor.

The floor to the boxed-in playhouse was a shelf, suspended and built high enough that the hood of our '42 blue Chevy found refuge under it. A plywood wall enclosed the shelf, and a back window looked out to the alley and gave the playhouse light.

To get up to the platform, I used a sturdy, six-foot wooden step ladder. I would face the ladder, hold onto its railing, and move one step at a time. Coming down from the playhouse, I descended in the same careful manner. I remember when I chose to go against this protocol and descended with my back to the ladder, facing outward to the yard. I don't know what happened in my descent. I could have missed a step or entangled a foot, but somehow, I must have fallen to the concrete floor below. The next thing I knew, I woke up in the guest room with my parents at my bedside, anxious for me to respond and show them I was alive. I learned my lesson. To this day, I always face the ladder, hold tightly to the sides, and go up and down, one careful step at a time.

In the playhouse was a doll bed, dresser, and refrigerator grandfather constructed for my sister. One day, during doll play, my friend Marilyn and I heard a strange noise out the window. "Marilyn, look at that man. He's confused, walking from one side of the road to the other, back and forth."

"Barbara, the man scares me. Let's call your mother. I think he needs help. Why is he in the alley?"

I was frozen in place, and yet, I wanted to run and tell mother about this strange behavior. I felt conflicted. Should I climb out of the playhouse and run to the house to tell my mother, or tuck the incident away and continue my play as if the man's condition did not exist? I don't remember what I did, but the man's behavior is a strong memory.

Outside the garage across the drive was an old, stately Black Walnut tree. It stood between the driveway and the Hasselman fence. Grandfather tied ropes to a tall branch, placed a hand-carved wooden bench for a seat, and I had a swing. I pumped hard and strong; my feet digging a crescent-shaped pit under the swing as my feet flew high above fence level. I felt as though I was taking flight above the garage.

Our gravel driveway offered me my first entrepreneurial adventure. The stones in the drive were just the right size to use as a medium for art painting. Finding my mother's bright red nail polish, I put the two together, made various designs, and soon had an inventory. Carrying my play table and chair to the end of the drive facing the front walk, I sat at the table, allowing space for foot traffic on the city sidewalk. One to two cents seemed a reasonable price. I don't remember making a first sale, but I do remember stubbing my toe and crying with pain. Father carried me inside the house for bandaging, then went back out and disassembled my stand. I wonder to this day if my parents shut down my enterprise because they were embarrassed by my business adventure. With more encouragement, I might have made a career in art or business. In sales, I later did well with Girl Scout Cookies and high school magazine subscriptions. Many years later, I sold metal sculptures, but I did not quit my day job.

5. Mother's Challenges

A ROTARY BLACK PHONE rested on a small round table in the dining room. RA (for Randolph) 5129 was easily memorized, and you dialed by placing your finger into the hole with the correct letter and number and rotating the disk. We had a Party Line. When placing a call, you lifted the receiver to see if the line were clear. In an emergency, if the line were occupied, you had to ask the other party to please hang up. What a pain.

In contrast to the sourpuss family at No. 51 was the Muth family at No. 36, four houses up the street. The Muth home was full of laughter as well as clutter. Gracie Muth was the kindest person I knew. She was also short and stocky. Mr. Muth smoked a cigar and laughed a lot. Tommy, their only kid, was my sister's age. Gracie taught me how to iron. When she saw me coming, she would remove the bulky ironing board from the closet, unhinge the squeaky metal legs, adjust the board to my waist height, and plug in the iron. My job was to press white handkerchiefs. Mr. Muth would tease me, interrupting my ironing concentration.

"Hey, you iron creases into my handkerchiefs, and Tommy's handkerchiefs are perfect. I think you favor Tommy!" We all laughed. It was true what he said, I did favor Tommy.

Gracie worked for the Memorial Park Cemetery and encouraged my father to buy plots in the Masonic section, which he did: six plots, one for each member of our family plus an extra for my brother's future wife. A few years later, when I was a sophomore in high school, my father died. We knew where he would be buried.

One snowy day in January, my mother sent me to the grocery store on Main Street to buy a loaf of bread. I had the correct change in my pocket, and I knew the route well. Past the Muth's, halfway up the street, on to Mrs. Heeter's at the corner of Fernwood and Main, then across the street to the store where bread sold for ten cents. A snowstorm was brewing, and while I was shopping, the snow turned into a blizzard.

Heading home, I pushed against a strong wind that resisted, making me feel as if I were pushing against a stubborn door not wanting me to enter. Tucking my chin to my chest and lowering my shoulders so that I was a compact force, my feet left deep grooves in the fresh powder. With my bread clutched in my hands, I reached our front porch and safety from the storm. I believe my mother sent me on that journey knowing that in life I would encounter many storms, and through persistence, purpose, and knowing, I would arrive at my goal. I would be able to find my way home.

Summer brought another journey. Mother sent me to Mr. Fleming's deli to buy ice cream cones. Mr. Fleming was our roomer, and his deli, on the corner of Kneckt Dr. and Main St., was next door to Mrs. Heeter's house. My task was to return to our house before the ice cream melted. Precious was the purchase! With the proper exchange of coins, I balanced five cones in a paper holder, and without getting distracted, hustled just enough to not spill the ice cream. I managed to get the cones home just as the first drip came down the side of the cone. Mother taught me timing and to focus on the task at hand.

The home at No. 49 Fernwood held many stories and treasured memories. Events and people shaped my early years with play time, adventure, confidence, and lots of love. The Golden Oak, Black Walnut, and two Sugar Maples will always occupy a giant and sacred place in my heart.

6. Small Adventures

Pennies. I slid a knife into the slot of my ceramic penny bank and turned the bank upside down, watching the pennies slide down the knife onto the table. Would I have enough to buy a present for my mother's birthday? I dumped what I had into a small brown paper bag and walked one block up the street to the grocery store. In the back of the store, on the right-hand side against the wall were items for the kitchen. I selected a thin plastic blue and white flowered tablecloth. It would be the perfect present, I thought. When I gave the storekeeper my handful of pennies, he counted them in front of me, smiled, winked, and said, "Just right."

Buttons. My mother, a teacher by training and an intense mother by vocation, sewed and mended our clothes. She kept the extra buttons—white buttons from old work shirts; covered buttons she made herself to match the garment she was constructing; dark buttons for men's pants; large decorative pearl buttons for coats; and tiny buttons difficult to handle—in a quart-sized Mason jar. Crowded together, one could see all the buttons at once. If you wanted the button in the middle of the jar, you had to dump all the buttons onto the table, but I enjoyed looking at each one as I put them back into the jar. I had a favorite dress my mother made me called "Buttons and Bows." I was wearing it when I broke my arm, trying to execute a backflip off the neighbor's gym set. Doctors at the hospital had to tear my button dress to cast my arm. The buttons and bows dress disappeared, and I never saw it again.

Childhood Movie Theater. Every Saturday morning, my parents dropped my sister, brother, and me off at the National Cash Register Company

16

auditorium, where the selected movie of the week was showing. I remember seeing the story of Bre'r Rabbit outwitting Bre'r Fox in Uncle Remus' "His Songs and His Sayings." When captured, Bre'r Rabbit said, "Do anything you want, but don't throw me into the briar patch." When we exited the movie theater, we were handed big, full-sized candy bars— Hershey's chocolate, Three Musketeers, or Snickers. Greedily, we tore off the paper and munched sweetness while looking for parents to pick us up.

Reflection 2021: I was a kid, enjoying the benefits of who I was, a descendent of European immigrants to the East Coast. I did not know that author Joel Chandler Harris' 1880 story of a fictional character of a rabbit was a folk tale of racial history of who controlled access to food and water, a story of racial injustice, a story of African Americans and White Supremacy.

Another movie theater night was Friday. Once a month, Father would take us to the Masonic Lodge, an impressive Romanesque-style temple which stood near the Renaissance-style Dayton Art Institute and nearby the Greek Orthodox Church. What I remember most about Friday night was the movie of Lassie. As a child on the farm, my mother had loved her Collie dog. Hearing mother's story and seeing Lassie, I have admired the Collie ever since as an animal of intelligence and beauty. I marvel still at the juxtaposition of three distinct architectures on a hill in Dayton overlooking the Miami River.

State and County Fair. Nothing can compare with the huge Ohio State Fair that covers many acres with farm animals, grange displays, the newest gadgets for slicing and dicing, beehives in action, the biggest and most up-to-date John Deere tractors, and plenty of hot dogs and fried donuts. But it's the Montgomery County Fair in Dayton that I remember most. Daddy and I would sit in the bleachers and watch the jumping horse competition.

With precision and grace, the horses would tuck their front legs and leap into the air, clearing the top bar. Their riders, in crisp equestrian suits, hats, and tall black shiny boots, bent close to the horse's necks and were partners in the jump.

Campfires. Junior high church and Girl Scout camps in the woods of Ohio were rites of passage. We were told stories of ancient Peoples, and that in prehistoric times, the campfires may have been those of the ancient Adena and Hopewell—Mound Builders of the Mississippi Valley. Along the banks of Bush Creek that meandered through the valley of Logan County, Serpent Mound was constructed on a cliff overlooking the creek and facing the summer solstice. Girl Scout Camp Whippoorwill was located near the mounds of Fort Ancient, halfway between Dayton and Cincinnati, and above dry creek beds filled with trilobite fossil rocks. In pre-glacial times, this area was once the bottom of a lake. Gazing into the flames as the night darkened around us, we contemplated the stories and sang camp songs, bringing the day to closure.

First Dance. In a long, full-circle, blue skirt; white, frilly short-sleeved blouse; black-and-white saddle shoes with white socks; scrubbed face; and blushing pink cheeks, I took my position in a long line of fourth-grade girls. Facing us across the gym floor were ruddy-faced fourth-grade boys. Mrs. Gettles was conducting a physical education class, teaching us square dancing. The boys always wanted to be partnered with peppy, freckled-face Priscilla Willis, and the girls wanted handsome Ronnie Lewis. But we took the next in line. Hand in hand, the partners stepped into the center of the floor and formed squares of four couples. The dance began.

Canada. My father was born in Uxbridge, in the province of Ontario, Canada, on June 1, 1890. Each year when I was young, our family vacation was spent traveling from Dayton to Niagara Falls, New York, and staying over in the rooming house across from the Nabisco factory, where we toured for fresh shredded wheat biscuits and triscuits, warm and crunchy right off the conveyor belts. Father took us for a ride on a cable car, hanging high above the whirlpool in the Niagara River. We wore raincoats to step into the caves under Niagara Falls, and rode the Maid of the Mist, a boat cruising close to the falls. In Uxbridge, on the Canadian side of the river, at the home of daddy's relatives, I sat in an old Mexican saddle with my feet stretching to touch the stirrups.

"You can have that saddle when your feet reach the stirrups," they said. It was the last time I saw the beautiful saddle, but I never forgot the promise. My grandparents owned land next to the Tuscarora Indian Reservation, and I remember father driving the car down reservation road. We'd wave to tribal families sitting on their front stoops.

Reflection 2021: Gone is the grandparent's land, acquired through eminent domain by the state of New York for a power station. Gone is the Mexican saddle. Gone is my father. The memories are not gone, stored until the time I can share them with grandchildren.

Interest in the ancient Mound Builders of the Mississippi Valley has accompanied my journey throughout life; I often return as a pilgrimage to Serpent Mound. In 2010, I travelled to Chichén Itzá in Mexico to see the Mayan temples and believe there is a connection between the Mayan and Mound Builders.

7.Threatening Encounter

1950

DURING MOTHER'S MIAMI UNIVERSITY OF OHIO DAYS, she was voted the perfect model —slender, athletic, blond, blue-eyed. She threw the javelin and the shot-put, qualifying as a recipient for her college letter sweater. Although she was asked to stay on at the university's sister college, Western College for Women, and teach chemistry, mother left the campus to teach high school in Portsmouth, a town on the Ohio River. She purchased the first Model-T Ford in Pike County to drive to work. In the seventeen years between college graduation, teaching, marriage, birthing my two siblings, and up to the time I was born, she put on weight. I never knew my mother to be the college model. I knew her only as a large, powerful woman. She wore sizes 42, 46, and 48 in dresses, and over the years attended Weight Watchers. Mother never lectured me, but when she spoke, it was direct and strong, and I listened. I absorbed her teachings without question. I don't know how old I was when she made this statement to me, but it got stuck somewhere in my brain, and there it forever resided. "We do not talk about sex."

When I was eight years old and in the third grade, the Brownie Scouts were on a field trip to Taylorsville Dam, one of the five dams built around Dayton in a conservancy district after the 1917 flood. In the adjoining park, the troop set up for a picnic and a worthwhile badge project. I needed to go to the bathroom, so the troop leader said I could go with a buddy. My friend Marilyn and I walked through the woods to the sheltered bathroom which had no doors on the toilet stalls. I had my pants down and sitting on the toilet when a big man walked through the open door. I jumped from the toilet and pulled up my pants to run. The man grabbed me and lifted me in the air. One arm was around my waist and one around my mouth. I struggled and kicked to be free. I succeeded and fled out the door to join Marilyn. We ran back to the troop. I said nothing. Not to our leaders or the other Brownie Scouts. I did not report the incident.

Two days later, my mother asked me to talk to her about the incident. Marilyn told her mother who told my mother. Mom talked with the troop leader to get clarity, but since the troop leader had not been informed, she was surprised to hear of the incident.

"Why did you not report this incident to your troop leader?" Mom asked me.

"You told me not to talk about sex and that's what I thought it was."

Mother and I had a simple, grown-up, brief, and business-like conversation. "Please tell me if something like this happens again."

Although it had been two days since the incident, law enforcement people scoured the park for the perpetrator. No one was found.

8. On stage

1951

LERA RAY'S DANCE STUDIO was on First Street in downtown Dayton, past the Presbyterian Church my family attended. Mother taught me how to use the bus to get from North Riverdale into town for Thursday's afternoon dance class. Whether ballet, tap, or toe, each class was preparing for the annual review, which would be presented before an audience of proud and anxious parents. The night of the review, my tap class began our well-practiced routine entering from stage left, all in unison, one behind the other like kindergarten line-up. Giving us our cue and playing on the grand piano in the orchestra pit, Mrs. Zebrowski struck the opening chords. We had practiced this entrance many times in the studio. But this time, in a live performance, we held our breath, letting the routine parade through our minds as our feet acted with muscle memory: Tap, tap, shuffle ball change. Repeat. Repeat. We moved in three separate circles, then formed five straight lines. Tap, tap, shuffle ball change. Shuffle ball change. Bring the leg in, kick out, shuffle, shuffle, shuffle ball change. Our costumes caught the spotlight and swayed with each shuffle.

Mother was the master costume sewer having worked through many a recital. I was now the second daughter to go through dance classes, and this annual June recital was the culmination of a school year's work of precision. The costume Mom made was short-sleeved and from a white satin fabric with large green polka dots. A sewed-in slit in the sleeves gave me space for arm movement. The skirt was short and barely covered my upper legs. It had a green silky fringe that shimmered as it picked up the spotlight.

We were through our routine of tapping, shuffling, and glimmering. Our parents were proud. The adulation was evident as the crowd rose to their feet, clapped, and whistled. We dancers spread our arms wide, locked arms, and in unison tapped forward to stage front. Mrs. Zebrowski hit a strong chord on the piano, and we bowed to our admirers. Glad that it was over, we picked up the pace and turned to stage right. In unison, one behind the other—with a tap, tap, shuffle ball change, repeat, repeat—we tapped until we were safely absorbed behind the curtain. We knew we were fabulous.

9. Miss Spring

1952

I WAS IN LOVE with my fourth-grade writing teacher, Miss Pauline Spring. She was fresh, eager, smiling, and made us work hard. She wore long, full, print-flowered skirts that smelled of springtime, and she moved around the classroom to the rhythm of a waltz, bringing us into her dance, and we not minding the difficulty of the step. Miss Spring instructed us properly:

"The intent of this writing exercise is to practice cursive, allowing the flow of the ink to move above and below the lines of the paper or resting on the lines themselves, distinct and clear, like a thin black snake crawling back and forth, up, and down, circling to connect itself. Hold your pen gently between your thumb and index finger and resting on the middle finger. Allow the ink to flow gently without pressing. Correct your posture when writing, sitting tall and proud."

I dipped my cork-ribbed pen with its removable metal tip into the black ink bottle, held securely in the round hole of the student desk. I felt like John Hancock with his feathered quill, proudly displaying his name for all of history to study. There would be no question as to whose signature was on the Declaration of Independence. Cursive was an art form, destined to make a statement with beauty and purpose.

The spell of love for Miss Spring was broken as the class moved on to fifth grade, then sixth, seventh, eighth, and on to high school. Miss Spring had somewhere among those years become a Mrs. Somebody. The ink bottles were replaced with pens that held their own ink. And now, years from fourth grade, I teach college students who often sign their papers with a wavy line that looks like a snake wiggling to its prey. In current student's press for learning, there is little time for careful penmanship, patiently crafted. Learning cursive has been dropped from the curriculum.

Years later, I will remember Miss Spring and her instruction of cursive writing when my co-mediator Paul in a session with the Dispute Resolution Center, proudly announced, "I will do the writing for the mediation agreement because I was taught cursive by the Catholic nuns." I examined his handwriting and indeed, he took the letters above and below the line, moving vowels and consonants across the page in a beautiful style, easily read. I let him do the writing that day and wondered if his Catholic nuns waltzed into the classroom as did Miss Spring.

10. My Father's Last Thanksgiving

1957

FOUR LEAVES WERE INSERTED INTO THE MAHOGANY TABLE, stretching it to its full length. Mother's white linen tablecloth, saved for family gatherings, was flipped open and edged into place. The fine silver chest was removed from its storage in the buffet, and forks, knives, and spoons were properly placed. Freshly laundered and pressed white linen napkins were placed to the left of the forks. Crystal goblets, used only on holiday, were placed at each setting. From the kitchen came aromas of a roasting turkey and a feast in progress. Mom mashed potatoes with melted butter and warm milk. Sister made green bean casserole with mushroom soup and fried onion rings. Baked sweet potatoes were sautéed in butter and brown sugar. Succotash, a combination of lima beans and corn, was heated. Jellied cranberry sauce was pushed from the can with the ridges intact. Pickles and a relish tray were set out in an oblong cut-glass dish. Homemade pumpkin, minced meat, apple, and southern pecan pies were cooling on the rack.

My sister Carolyn, brother Jerry, and Brian, one of Jerry's fraternity brothers came from the university for the weekend holiday. Grandmother Josie and her sister Great Aunt Callie Maude Marks were living with us. My beloved grandfather was missing. He had died at our home the previous March. Mother, father, and I added three more to the dinner table, a total of eight for Thanksgiving weekend. It was appropriate that we had welcomed a guest into the family gathering. There was room for all, using the three bedrooms upstairs, with my father being bumped to an army cot in the basement rec room.

"We gather together to ask the Lord's blessing." The meal began with singing the traditional Thanksgiving hymn. Mother asked we go around the table and each of us say for what we were most thankful. Grandmother Josie, the eldest, began, "I am thankful that this old table is once again opened for a family gathering."

Great Aunt Cal continued, "Each Thanksgiving is a blessed family event, from the history of our pioneer ancestors in the horse and buggy era, to modern times. With the help of the auto, we travel to be together. And I am pleased to bake the pies."

"I am thankful to be away from campus where everyone is uptight about final exams," spoke my sister.

"Hey, give us your blessings on those finals," said brother. "My head is filled with formulas and mathematical equations."

Brian joined in. "I am thankful that I could be a part of your family gathering and to get to know you. It is a lovely break from studies, and it all looks to be delicious as well."

With tears in his eyes, my father spoke tenderly. "I am proud of my daughter studying English at the university and my son becoming an engineer."

I was watching my father's shirt; I was sure he was going to "bust his buttons." He looked across the table, smiled, and said, "And my youngest is going to be a nurse and take care of me in my old age."

I was next. "I am glad Carolyn, Jerry, and Brian are here. I have missed them, and it feels good to be a complete family around the table."

Mother, missing her own father at the table this year, said, "We are blessed that the students have returned, and the family has gathered for

Thanksgiving. May we remember my father and those not at the table this year and remain strong and healthy to return another year."

In grateful unison, we toasted, "To the feast." After the meal, feeling satisfied and satiated, the family and guest complimented the chefs, saying together, "This is the best Thanksgiving ever."

Too soon, it was our last day together. Sunday morning, we filed into the long wooden pews of the Gothic-style Westminster Presbyterian Church, where my father served as an Elder. The magnificent Tiffany stained-glass window channeled streams of red, blue, and purple onto the chancel while we listened to the organist's prelude, a Bach cantata. After lunch, the three university folks got rides with friends and headed back to campus in two separate cars. In the evening, I attended youth fellowship, and Paul, one of the guys who brought me home, walked me up to the door. Daddy opened it.

"Hey, come on in. Look at today's paper. The Russians launched Sputnik! This is exciting news." My father, who had long been interested in flight and had worked with Orville Wright on the Dayton Community Board, was impressed with the exploration into space.

Paul regretted he had to get home. "Thanks. Space travel is interesting, but I got to go home and do my homework. Monday comes quickly after a holiday weekend. Good night."

"I think I'll head upstairs and get ready for bed," I announced. I needed to place large, pink, squishy rollers in my hair to make my straight hair curly. I passed through the living room and noticed the front page of the *Dayton Daily News* laid out on the ottoman; its headline featured Sputnik.

Daddy spoke, rather pensively, "I'm not feeling well; I think I'll turn in early. Perhaps, it's indigestion." He tentatively climbed the steps to the second-floor bedroom. "Barbara, would you please run to the basement and get my pajamas? I left them on the cot in the rec room."

"Of course, Daddy. I'll be right back, won't take long." In the time it took for me to descend two flights of stairs and then climb back to the second floor, something was terribly wrong. Daddy had fallen across the bed and was unconscious. I yelled downstairs.

"Momma, help! Come quickly." Mother hustled up the steps, saw my father, reached for the phone, and called the fire department. Almost immediately, we heard the sirens, loud and clear in the fall night air. Mom called Kenny Kurtz, Daddy's physician, who said he was on his way. Grandmother cried. She and I waited in her bedroom where we could hear the confusion but stayed out of the way of the firemen, physician, and mother, who were anxiously attending to my father. I was scared. Grandma and I hugged each other and sobbed.

"There was nothing else you could have done," Dr. Kurtz reassured mother.

In the shocked silence of sudden death, mother reached again for the phone and called her sorority sister, who with her husband, owned the local funeral home. Looking out the front window, I saw the white-sheet-draped body cart being carried down the uneven fossilized front steps to the waiting hearse.

My world was diminished. I was a teen, fifteen years old, a sophomore in high school, knowing all there was to know at this age, believing the world existed for me. I was not mature enough to have had talks with my father about life and love. Now, there would be no father-daughter chats. Without warning, my father was gone. Sunday evening on Thanksgiving weekend, December 1, 1957. I remember.

11. Service Station Attendant

1959

MY BROTHER WAS BEGINNING A JUNIOR YEAR INTERNSHIP for his chemical engineering course at a northern Ohio paint factory. Mother asked me to drive his old car home from Evanston, Illinois to Dayton, a trip of six hours. The old car, slowly dying of debilitation and rust, had two quirks that needed fixing. When the car stopped, it sometimes had trouble starting again, a symptom of old age. And the handle of the passenger side of the car did not open from the inside. It worked when entering the car from the outside, but not the reverse. The passenger had to exit the car by sliding over the gear shift and out the driver's side or, be let out by the driver.

I felt important at seventeen and a junior in high school. I knew I was competent to make the trip, and family trusted me. Mom had taught me to drive, and I did well with parallel parking. Getting in a car, heading down the highway on my own gave me the feeling of freedom and power.

Roadside rest stations provided the breaks I needed, but always with the anxiety of *Will my car start again if I stop?* Three hours into the road trip, I pulled off the highway into a service station to fill up. I kept the car running and spoke to the mechanic about the trouble I was having with getting the car started again once it had stopped. Could he check on that, please? He said he would drive it a piece and listen to the motor. I scooted over to the passenger seat and allowed him to climb into the driver's seat.

Across the road from the service station was the county racetrack, grandstands, and barns. The area looked abandoned as there was nothing scheduled this time of year. The mechanic pulled forward from the pumps, checked the traffic on the main road, and drove across the road into the racetrack property. So far, the car was behaving. He drove up a dirt road that ran next to the racetrack, pulled up to a secluded spot behind one of the barns, and shut the engine off. He turned to me, but his mind was not on the car engine.

I did some quick calculations. He didn't know I could not escape from my side of the car, and I did not want to be alone with him in this deserted spot. He was bigger than I was. I did have a voice, and I could put some effort behind it. I spoke firmly, directly, slowly, pulling out the words so that he could clearly hear my intent.

"Get -- This -- Car -- On -- The -- Road!"

Slowly, he turned back to the driver's position, shrugged his shoulders, and started the engine. I said a silent thank you to the car for backing me up. He pulled out of the secluded spot and followed the racetrack back to the filling station. When he stepped out of the car, I slid over to the driver's seat, put the car on the road, and did not stop until I arrived in Dayton. This time, I told my mother what happened. An appointment was made at the auto repair shop the next day. The engine was checked, and the handle on the passenger side was promptly repaired.

12. Suitcase

1960

"THIS IS THE LATEST FASHION IN SUITCASES; I wanted you to look smart leaving home for college," Mother said. She was proud of her investment in my high school graduation gift: a four-piece grey Samsonite luggage set, consisting of a large, a medium, and a small pullman, plus a sturdy train case complete with mirror.

"Gosh, mom, it's handsome. I'm going to school in style!" I remembered my grandfather's black, worn leather "grip" as he called it. It had a strong metal latch that clicked into place and two heavy leather straps with strong buckles to reinforce the latch. He never left home without his grip. Mother started reminiscing when she left home for college. I remember when my brother Harold took me to Miami University in Oxford, Ohio, in 1921. He left my trunk and me at the college gate. Everything I owned was in that trunk. Although my brother was older than I by three years, I was the first in my family to go to college. I was alone and scared.

Now, thirty-five years after my mother was left at the college gate, I am making the same move. History is made by people who for centuries have left their homes and traveled to distant cities. They've said goodbye to parents, shouldered their belongings, turned their faces into the future, and stepped forward. The suitcase is more than a vessel of belongings; it's a symbol of passage. My mother was a quiet person, but if she were more vocal, I think she might have said this: "I fill your suitcase with love. Believe in your potential to learn. Allow yourself to venture into the unknown. Cut your own path through the wilderness of life. Never be

GIRL FROM DAYTON

afraid to leave home, to pack your suitcase again and again, to move on in new directions, and to learn. Enjoy the journey and go with love."

I might have responded: "Thank you, mother, for the true meaning of suitcase, packing in the lessons of life will give me strength and courage on the journey. I love you."

Gripping my suitcases, I left home.

33

13. Photographs – Girl from Dayton

I was a happy baby, knew love, and lived in a contented neighborhood.

Growing up in Dayton.

Uncle Jimmy, my father's brother, of Uxbridge, Canada. I loved him dearly.

On stage we were fabulous.

In the fifth-grade high jump event on May Field Day, I managed to clear the bar at 45 inches, but landed on my leg in a heap upon the mat. I broke the leg in four places. Nancy Banta had longer legs, and I was sure she would win. However, the event was ended, and Nancy and I tied for first place. We both received blue ribbons.

With broken leg.

The Coronel White High School cheerleaders. I am top row between Terri and Pat. Beth is far right. Riding on the band bus and cheerleading for football games was fun.

II. Ken and Barbara

1965-1976

WHEN THE MATTEL DOLLS HIT THE MARKET in the sixties, everyone talked about the good-looking couple Ken and Barbie. They were popular role models.

14. Love

LIKE ELEMENTS IN COLLEGE CHEMISTRY CLASS, we were attracted to each other. There he was—handsome, clean cut, short hair, twinkly eyes, and a husky voice. A long tweed coat with the collar turned up to protect his neck, covered his tall frame. He wore a black nubby wool Russian-type hat on his head.

"Hey, may I walk you back to the dorm?" he asked.

"Yes, that would be nice," I responded.

My heart was leaping ahead of my step. Or I was stepping slower to make the walk last longer. It was autumn in Ohio. As we walked, we kicked up crunchy leaves just to see them fall again and smell their musky crispness. We crossed the quadrangle and walked past Mirror Lake until we reached the nursing dorm on Tenth Avenue. The chemistry between us was mingling.

Ken was a handsome fraternity man who provided weekend social activities and a break from the demands of an intense nursing curriculum. Yet, he was not my one and only date. There were too many others to not explore the possibilities of new relationships away from Dayton and the eyes of a protective mother.

Rich traveled on a Greyhound bus from California to enroll at Ohio State. He'd walk me to early morning clinical at University Hospital. I still have the lovely poetry he wrote to me tucked in a secret box in the attic. Larry, a cheery red-headed frat man who had a spring in his step and who kept me laughing, was a serious contender. Joe was a medical student and tennis partner.

In my fourth and last year of college, I decided to take summer quarter off and spent the weeks as a Girl Scout camp counselor, leading biking trips on back roads by Amish farms with red barns, fertile farms, and grazing cattle. I taught the girl scouts synchronized swimming and cooked lovely stew spiced with turmeric and curry over an open campfire with my East Indian co-counselor. It was Ken who drove me back and forth from camp sessions. By the end of that summer, I was ready to return to a disciplined surgical unit to complete requirements for a degree in nursing practice and sit for my exams to be a registered nurse. I was ready to make a choice on my dates, and it was Ken who became my steady.

My roommate, suitemate, and another Delta Zeta Sorority sister planned their weddings to follow graduation. I was to be a bridesmaid in all three weddings. Ken was a groomsman in one. We began to think we might be married too. While ballroom dancing late one night, he held me close and whispered, "Barbara, I love you. Will you marry me?" As I looked into his eyes, I thought of my three friends who married the year before. My biological clock was ticking. I was living at home with my mother to save money and pay off the Volkswagen. Ken and I had been discussing our future and had been ring shopping. His question was well timed. "Yes," I responded. Ken pulled from his pocket the set-at-an-angle sparkly diamond ring we had earlier seen at Mr. Gile's jewelry store. I laid my head on his chest as we continued to waltz around the ballroom floor under a flashing strobe light. The music was tender and romantic, and we relaxed into happy thoughts of what our future would bring.

15. Wedding Gown Borrowed

1965

I WENT LOOKING FOR A WEDDING DRESS, and after trying on dress after dress, my sister's beaded and lace-sleeve organza was still the most beautiful. Besides, I was used to having hand-me-downs. I asked if she would let me wear her dress for "something borrowed." My brother would take the place of my father and walk me down the aisle. For the bridesmaids' dresses, I chose emerald, green silk fabric for a sleeveless sheath pattern. The green dress would be belted with a royal blue velvet ribbon at the waist and a matching ribbon in the hair. Each bridesmaid would construct her own dress and carry a bouquet of blue button straw flowers. On August 28, 1965, exactly one year to the date of my graduation from the Ohio State University, Ken and I were married in the Westminster Presbyterian Church in downtown Dayton. Under the exquisite Tiffany-stained glass window, with the sun's rays streaming down upon us, we repeated our vows.

The blue VW "bug," became our get-away car. As we pulled away from the church, with cans rattling behind, our photo was snapped with a background tire store sign across the street, *Dayton Thorobreds*. We drove south to Cincinnati and crossed the Ohio River into Kentucky, enjoying the drive, having long since removed the clanky cans. Tired and happy, we chatted easily. In what is known as bluegrass country, we arrived at the Lexington Inn. The stone fountain and circular drive to the front door gave the impression of elegance. Here, as newlyweds and virginal lovers, we would consecrate our union.

To be confident I was ready for my wedding night, Dr. Barr, my gynecologist, prescribed medication that helped me relax. When ready, I took the medication, which required twenty minutes to take effect. We set a timer. Watching the minutes move ever so slowly, we counted down. "Sex with your partner is like being a violinist who plans to be a virtuoso," Dr. Barr counseled in a premarital session. "You keep practicing making it perfect." It all came together, and I was in ecstasy. I thought that if sex were this good on our first night, think of how it would be when we keep practicing! I was looking forward to the rest of our honeymoon, and beyond.

We dressed and went to breakfast in the elegant dining room. I was self-conscious and felt everyone must be looking at me. Was it obvious that it had been my wedding night? Could they tell by the smile on my face? I realized they didn't care and were not interested. After breakfast, we packed the car to head south to Gatlinburg, Tennessee, and the great Smoky Mountains.

Reflection 2021: A side story of that happy, get your marriage started, a time so long ago...Proud of both her millinery and sewing skills, mother constructed my going away outfit, which included a blue-flowered box hat that matched the dress fabric. During our honeymoon travels, my new husband Ken sought every opportunity to allow a suitcase to fall accidentally and smash the hat beyond recognition but resisted the temptation. The homemade matching fabric pillbox hat remained unscathed. Yet, today, I cannot remember what became of it.

16. Within Mist and Fog on the Appalachian Trail

"HONEY, THERE'S A CANCELLATION at LeConte Lodge on the Appalachian Trail, and they said we could have the reservation for three days," Ken informed me. This was great news. We would leave Gatlinburg and hike the trail to the mountain lodge.

"Where do we leave the car?" I asked.

"We can park at the trailhead, putting only what we need in our backpacks," Ken replied. "It could take us four hours to climb the Alum Cave route, but it will be worth it." We packed thoughtfully. Whatever we packed, we had to carry on our backs, so we concentrated on the Ten Essentials: water, map, compass, sunglasses and sunscreen, extra clothing, headlamp or flashlight, first-aid supplies, matches, knife, and extra food.

We arrived at the trailhead, slipped our backpacks in place, and signed the trail log. It was early September, and the air held the musky, sweet smell of autumn. The maple, oak, and ginkgo trees of Gatlinburg boasted gold, red, orange, and crispy brown. Eager to begin, we stepped into the forest and were immediately covered by a lush canopy of color. We were among very few on the trail and walked in silence and reverence as we hiked among old growth trees. It was as if the forest understood and welcomed us into their community, encouraging us on our way.

"Honey, I'm looking forward to being at the top for a few days. I want us to see the sunset and the sunrise on Lookout Point," Ken said.

"Sounds beautiful and romantic." I responded. Talk was easy, sporadic, and in rhythm with our pace, interrupted occasionally for water and GORP (*Good Old Raisins and Peanuts*), but today refers to any trail mix, usually dried fruits, and nuts).

Three hours later, the deciduous trees thinned. The temperature dropped, and we pulled sweaters from our packs. Evergreens of pine and fir became companions. A damp mist floated in the air and shrouded the trees. We pulled rain jackets from our backpacks. The air became like a cotton cloud. As we climbed higher, mist became fog. From our packs came gloves and knit hats. We continued to climb. As the trail leveled to a plateau, we began to distinguish the outline of roofs and faint voices through the fog. Relieved to have made it to our destination, we checked in at the reception desk in the main cabin.

"Welcome to Mt. Le Conte Lodge. Here is your stack of firewood, your bucket of water, and towels. Your cabin is number seven, over there in the woods. The bathrooms are communal, just across the way."

Ken started a fire in the pot-bellied iron stove with a large exhaust pipe that looked like a fat cobra coiling through the roof. The receptionist provided newspapers and matches as a fire start. Ken placed the bucket of water on the stove knowing it would take a while to heat because of our mountain elevation, but we looked forward to getting a start on our baths. I laid out my trousseau. This rustic cabin high in the mountains, together with the smell of the forest and the warmth from the crackling fire, made a lovely honeymoon suite.

17. Peace Corps Training

1966

INSPIRED BY THE WORDS OF PRESIDENT JOHN F. KENNEDY, "Ask not what your country can do for you, but what you can do for your country," Ken and I applied to the U.S. Peace Corps. In April, we flew to Vermont to train at the Experiment in International Living at Brattleboro. Eight hours a day, six days a week, we focused on learning Portuguese. Ten professors from Brazil drilled us in the language and taught Brazilian culture, manners, and how to live in small towns throughout the country. Ken, who spoke French, and volunteers who spoke other languages such as Russian, Italian, Spanish, and German, were the most proficient language learners. I was in group number ten, the bottom group. My high school Latin class with Miss Ruth Koontz did not adequately prepare me for learning Portuguese. I was anxious my lack of language facility would cause me to be "deselected."

Each of the volunteers brought different skills, which we taught to each other. Rich led calisthenics at 6:00 in the morning. Sue and John taught us how to be teachers. Jim from Nebraska helped us learn how to farm. We raised three goats and three pigs, naming the pigs for our esteemed psychologists who were observing our mental fitness to serve. I taught health care and how to administer injections.

One spring weekend, a hundred volunteer trainees were left in communities throughout New England with the assignment of analyzing the economics, history, religion, and culture of the town and reporting back when we returned to the training site. Our trainers gave us $12.50 each. In our designated town, Rutland, Vermont, Ken and I walked the

45

streets for hours, studied the names in the phone book, analyzed the businesses. When at dusk we needed a place for the night, we approached the Episcopal Church and requested lodging. Father Webster and his wife Kate invited us into their home. As their guests, we became kitchen servers for the congregational dinner, met the mayor of the town, and learned the town's history, culture, and economy by listening to the stories of those working in the kitchen.

By the end of the weekend, volunteers could report that they now knew life in New England towns, and few of us had spent our allotment. For his lodging, one volunteer reported spending two nights in the city jail. The entire group had connected with townsfolk, listened to stories, learned history and ethnicity, and shared cultures. In return, the townspeople took care of us. People to people, in the world together, caring to know each other.

18. A Sense of Place

OUR FIRST HOME IN BRAZIL was a white house with a blue door and hard-packed clay floors. It was on the corner of a village park called a *praça*, catty-cornered from the Catholic church in a small town called Ibicaraí in the southern region of the state of Bahia in Brazil. The house had a front window that allowed for air circulation to move as in a railroad car home— in the window, through the front room, dining room, into the kitchen, and out the back door. Every day, I opened the door and the window to the sunshine. I dampened down and lightly swept the clay floor. The bedroom was off the dining room and had just enough space for a double-sized wooden frame bed with a lumpy mattress, mosquito netting, and one chest of drawers. Over the dining room table, a light bulb on a long cord hung from the rafters.

From the Saturday morning open market in the town square, I purchased a hand woven, round, reed basket with a lid. Turned upside down, the basket served as a lamp shade for the naked bulb, and its lid became our breadbasket. To cover the plastered wall of the dining room with a bit of interest, I attached the covers of Time magazines that we had received in the mail, dated July 1966 to November 1968. One Time cover, at eye level, was George Herbert Walker Bush, head of the CIA.

In the kitchen, I managed to acquire a propane stove, even though the built-in, charcoal-burning concrete stove was cheaper and safer to use, especially when I put my black beans on to cook before I left in the morning for the medical clinic. The *quintal* (backyard garden) had a functioning well, which served not only for drawing water but as a gathering place for those who wanted to observe the Americans at home. The outdoor privy was also in the back of the quintal and consisted of a concrete slab with a hole in it, placed over a large pit and surrounded by an enclosed wooden shack. A *loofah* bush on the fence at the back door provided us with dish and bath scrubs. The kitchen had a rough worktable where vegetable scraps would be dumped out the open, screenless window above the table. The chickens in my neighbor's *quintal* on the other side of the window appreciated the shaved carrot and potato peels.

Our house stood on a cobblestone street, carefully laid by workmen's hands in the hot sun. Extended lunch breaks kept their bodies from the hottest part of the day as they retreated under palm trees to eat lunch, consisting mostly of left-over black beans mixed with *farofa*—rough and grainy *farina* (flour), which had been sautéed in a little butter, salt, pepper, and a few chopped green peppers, tomatoes, and fresh cilantro. If the men could afford it, a fresh tropical fruit would be added, frequently one of the varieties of bananas: small finger banana, red banana, boiled plantain, * or *banana de prata*—a common table banana we eat in the States.

On Friday afternoons, these cobblestone streets took on a rodeo-style atmosphere as steers were driven cowboy style to the butcher shops in town, slaughtered in anticipation for the next day's market. Saturday Market, the most exciting time of the week, became the meeting place for people coming in from the *campo* (countryside) to see, buy, trade, and visit. I could buy a strip filet of beef, hand-crafted wooden spoons, hand-built clay pots, and select the plumpest among the scrawny chickens and have a friend slaughter it for me. In the market, I visited with friends and neighbors, stocked up on fresh vegetables, and purchased eggs, which I carried in a wire basket. Milk, fresh from the campo, was taken to market in large cans on the backs of burros. We purchased the milk in liters, took it home to boil on the propane stove, and poured it into our cups of evening coffee. There was common knowledge that boiling milk prevented bovine tuberculosis, but boiling water for the prevention of disease was a much harder sell. Having no refrigeration, our Saturday supplies dwindled through the week. By the following Friday evening, we ate an egg, toast, and coffee and would, once again, be looking forward to market to replenish our supplies.

Ken's community development work

ONE OF KEN'S TASKS was to build the local Boy Scout organization. His uniform consisted of shorts, a khaki short-sleeved shirt, and a neck scarf with an emblem of the international Boy Scout movement. Ken assisted when the local troop conducted a campout by the school on the hill overlooking the town. He trained the fathers to take over so that he could slip out of leadership when the time came for our departure.

Ken's most important work, however, was the literacy program he promoted through his mentorship with Luiz Barbosa Santos. Based on Paulo Freire's book, *Pedagogy of the Oppressed*, Luiz organized a local education program to teach the workers to read and write. Freire's program was called *Alfabetização*, which means literacy in Portuguese. Freire was the former Brazilian Secretary of Education whose philosophy and activism were to teach literacy at the grass roots level. These teachings, however, did not sit well with ruling politicians, and Freire had been exiled from Brazil. He went to Chile where literacy was a national priority. Freire later went to the United States where he taught at Harvard. Near the end of his life, Paulo Freire returned to Brazil. If the people of Ibicarai could read and write, they could vote. If they could vote, they would help build their community.

Luis had the equivalent of a fifth-grade education. Understanding the power of education and with Ken's mentorship, Luis invited *professoras* (teachers) who had graduated from the *ginásio* (8th grade) to teach in ten school classrooms across town. The mayor provided support by opening school buildings at night. At the end of a long day in the *cacao* groves, men came to learn. After a day washing laundry in the river, women came to learn. In shirts and dresses, freshly pressed with charcoal heated heavy hand irons, the students walked tall, proud to attend. Ken remained in the background as Luis' coach.

Ken understood gíria, the local slang, language of the streets. He was always ready to join the troubadours when they passed the house. He often spent the evening drinking and singing, arriving home long after I had crawled under the mosquito netting.

Barbara's clinic and public health work:

I REPORTED AT 8:00 AM TO THE HEALTH CLINIC of *SESP, Serviço Especial de Saúde Público*, the national public health agency responsible for delivering health care to the community. The first task was to triage those who had walked miles to see the doctor. As head nurse of the clinic, I supervised the midwives who assisted birthing women in their homes, offering them sterile supplies and the chance to network and learn. I worked also with the *visitadoras*, nurse aides, who walked to the campo to see new mothers and remind them of their follow-up maternity visits at the clinic and obtaining the infant's immunizations.

There were health issues in Ibicaraí. Our landlady, Dona Joanna, a respected midwife, told us the story of an event that happened the night before we arrived in town. A woman in labor suffered when her placenta detached from the wall of the uterus before the delivery of the baby, a condition known as placental abruption. Because this was an emergent situation, the hospital was forty miles away, the woman lived in a barro with no transportation and no electricity, the woman and baby did not survive. Another story was of an untrained midwife who placed manure on the open umbilical cord as a ritual. The birthing woman contracted tetanus spores from the manure and died of lockjaw. I saw a woman walk past our door with her young son. She suffered from Elephantiasis, and one very swollen leg made walking painful. Her young son had an enlarged abdomen, which made him look like an adult American male with a six-pack belly. The child contracted intestinal parasites from walking barefoot in the dirt. One day, the health service came to turn our chairs upside down and spray our home with DDT as a preventive public health practice against malaria and chagas disease.

At the clinic, I began to see patients who came in with schistosomiasis—a disease also known as snail fever and bilharzia, caused by parasitic flatworms called schistosomes. Infected people, left untreated, can experience liver damage, kidney failure, infertility, or bladder cancer. Children could suffer from poor growth and learning disabilities. The schistosome perpetuates its life cycle in the calm waters of the river by penetrating the skin of the person who enters the river.

In the first few days of our residence, Netińha came for our laundry and carried the clothes to the river to join other laundry women who had gathered for their social connections. Children swam in the river's gentle waters. Dogs followed them, splashing behind the children.

"Netińha, you can't wash our clothes in the river. You'll get sick," I said.

"Dona Barbara, if I do not have your clothes to wash, I will find another client. I depend upon the pay for the work I do."

Ken and I were in conflict over the community's lack of safe water for washing clothes. Back in the States we had a central water system with automatic washing machines. Here, there was only a contaminated river. We could envision a central laundry area where the women could wash their clients' clothes but with safe well water. The laundry center would provide a gathering place for the women to work and socialize.

One day, I walked with the visitadoras to a distant barro. We were concerned that a new mother had not returned to the clinic for her twin babies' first immunizations. Upon arrival at her home, we learned that the babies had died. Shocked, we asked, "Why? How?"

"Diarreia," the mother said.

Diarrhea. One word. Dehydration. Another word. Had the mother, instead of breastfeeding, resorted to formula mixed with local water? Did the new mother not know to first boil and filter all water? In this part of the world, babies are often named only after they survived their first year. Sadly, the *visitadoras* and I returned to the clinic to rethink our nursing practices; we did not want this tragedy to happen again.

A young woman, Jací, came to our door one day and asked to work in community health care. Jací was in her twenties, a tall, slender, attractive woman with a rich brown complexion. Her mother was native Tupi-Guarani, and her father, of Portuguese heritage. Jací became our town's representative to the Public Health State Conference on Access to Health Care, where she spoke up about the lack of services in areas that were distant from the state capital. Coming from an interior town, her voice was credible, strong, direct, and powerful.

At the end of day, we would take our cups of evening coffee along with chairs and place them in front of the blue door to sit and relax with the neighbors. As the heat of the day dissipated, the vultures would begin their nightly circling in search of dinner. Ken called it, what sounded to us in local speak, *"Hora de Urubú"* (hour of the vulture). Dusk. Young couples, chaperoned by siblings, would begin to *passiar* in the park. Guitars were strummed, and songs filled the evening, a relaxed, happy time.

Our heavy suitcase-size, transoceanic radio brought us the British Broadcasting Company (BBC). We tuned in to the Democratic National Convention in Chicago with Mayor Richard Daly. President Lyndon Johnson had previously announced, "I shall not accept my party's nomination for president." Although it was evening in Ibicaraí, Ken and I rode our bicycles to the home of our town's mayor to tell him of the political chaos in Chicago.

Isolated from the tumult in the States and working co-operatively in a diverse community—descendants of Native First Peoples, Portuguese, former enslaved African Brazilians, immigrants of Lebanese and Syrian descent—Ken and I continued our work in literacy and health, hoping our work would contribute to community development.

Reflection 2021: Time magazines kept us informed of cities burning and assassinations. Ken and I were distant from the 1960s violence and hate within American cities, but we felt the tension across the continents and had to explain to our neighbors in language they could understand. "The long hot summer of 1967" was the name given to the 159 race riots that swept cities of the U.S. Among them, Detroit in which 7,000 National Guardsmen were brought in to restore order and 1,000 injured, 7,000 arrested, and 2,000 buildings damaged. In New York and New Jersey, 26 died, 1,500 injured, 1,000 arrested. There were race riots in Cairo, Illinois; Durham, North Carolina; Memphis, Tennessee; and Cambridge, Maryland. Four died in a race riot in Milwaukee. In June, '67, Muhammad Ali was sentenced to five years for draft evasion (later conviction overturned.) April 4, 1968, Martin Luther King, Jr. was assassinated in Memphis, TN, having previously received the Nobel Peace Prize for nonviolent protest. On June 6, 1968, Robert Kennedy, a Presidential candidate for our highest office was assassinated in California. The Beatles in July released "Sgt. Pepper's Lonely-Hearts Club" and "All You Need is Love." In August, 45,000 were sent to Viet Nam and Thurgood Marshall was confirmed as the first Black justice. The Best Picture of 1968 was "In The Heat of the Night" starring Sidney Poitier and Rod Steiger.

Folks have asked if plantain was a vegetable since I referred to it as a boiled banana in a workman's lunch. Plantain is a variety of banana high in starch and sugar. Dona Maria taught me to add it to the bean pot as a boiled vegetable. It also makes a tasty dessert when sliced lengthwise and sauteed in butter with added sugar and cinnamon.

19. Feijoada

SHORTLY AFTER MOVING INTO THE COMMUNITY, our next-door neighbor, Dona Maria, a slender woman with a cleft lip, taught me how to prepare *feijão*, black beans, the basis for feijoada, the national dish of Brazil. It was hard to understand Dona Maria's diction, as her cleft lip had not been surgically corrected, a medical resource not readily available in this small town on the edge of the *sertão*. Dona Maria was a slight woman who proudly stood as tall as Ken's chest. She wore a simple hand-sewn dress that hung loosely over slender legs. Her smile, twinkly eyes, excellent cooking demonstrations, and belief in my ability to learn Brazilian bean cooking, ensured success.

Black beans cooked in a clay pot, which had been hand-built by an elder whose slender, gnarly fingers shaped the sensual curvature. She crafted a lid with a ball-shaped handle on top which fit the pot perfectly. I loved to stroke the smooth sides of the pot and admire how it grew in character as the bottom turned black from the hot charcoal fire. I'd fill the pot with black beans and place it to simmer before I left for the clinic in the morning. At noon, when I returned home for lunch, I added chunks of squash and plantain to the beans, and in the last few minutes, slipped cabbage leaves under the lid to steam. Rice was prepared in a separate pan to which I added small pieces of green pepper, tomato, and cilantro.

When I passed the *paderia*, the baker removed two baguette-sized rolls from the oven, wrapped them loosely in a square of brown paper, and tied them with a thin string. After a substantial meal of rice, beans, and rolls, we rested before I returned to the clinic later in the afternoon.

20. Planned Parenthood

FAMILY PLANNING WAS A PRESSING NEED in our small Brazilian town, and I recall a few stories in which I was asked to intervene. Déte, our neighbor on the other side of the dirt road and two houses down from the praça, knocked on our open door:

"Do you have an aspirin? I am pregnant and cannot afford another child. My son Gilson is nine now, and he is enough. I want to lose this pregnancy. I swallowed my wedding ring. I hope it works."

Eight months later, Déte asked me to visit the stillborn infant she delivered during the night. I crossed the road and entered her home. The infant laid on top of the shuttle sewing machine table. I moved close to pay my respects. The infant looked like a tiny doll tenderly laid to nap. A midwife I did not know had attended the birth.

When she told me that Gilson would lead the procession to the cemetery, I did not know what to say, nor did I ask if this was the local custom when observing the rituals around a stillborn death. Without speaking, I tucked the scene away, wondering what had taken place in the night and if this outcome would have been different for Déte if she could have received the same level of maternal health services as the rich people in town who could purchase birth control pills from the local pharmacy. The scene has remained with me, and I return to its significance wherever there is a discussion of need for Planned Parenthood services.

A few months after the baby's death, a man on horseback rode up to our front window and knocked. He had ridden in from the campo, asking how to access family planning services. Unless he had the financial resources for the birth control pills in the pharmacy, I did not have a ready answer. When I tried to enlist the cooperation of four Italian nuns, serving in the church across the praça, the padre was not supportive and began a campaign discouraging my speaking to anyone about family planning. His campaign involved a public address system mounted on a jeep as he drove through town, blaring his concerns through a loudspeaker horn: "You will not use birth control. It is against the teaching of the Catholic Church. In our district, the bishop is the 15th child in the family."

The indigent needed equal access to family planning and reproductive services without discrimination on income. The indigent loved their children as much as the rich loved theirs but had fewer resources to ensure them a healthy life.

After Ken and I had been at our site for one full year, we took vacation. At this same time, the International Planned Parenthood Conference was convening in Santiago, Chile. It was 1967 and the conference would be held in Chile because the country was recognized as a leader in health care, literacy, and agricultural reform. Due to a high percentage of maternal deaths from illegal abortions at the hands of the untrained who were performing debaucheries on desperate women, the country offered medically safe abortions performed by professionally trained physicians. Chile was a world leader in reproductive maternal health care; the country provided access to all women. We traveled from Ibicaraí to Santiago.

Our trip took us south from Bahia on a slick Mercedes bus to Rio de Janeiro, then on to Curitiba and Porto Alegre in Brazil's southernmost state. Pelotas was the last large Brazilian city before crossing the border into Uruguay, where our immediate destination was Montevideo, the capital. We rested and sat with the statues in the main plaza before boarding a hydrofoil, skimming the waters of the Rio de la Plata, and docking in Argentina.

Buenos Aires is a garden city. Walks in the woodsy parks provided a respite. Our hotel had an open-air elevator with an iron frame cage that clinked and swayed as it slowly cranked us to the third floor. The atmosphere was European, in contrast to the *sertão* and Ibicaraí. The climate in Buenos Aires was temperate versus tropical in Bahia. We boarded a train which went from Buenos Aires to Mendoza, the wine country, and the foothills of the Andes. In Mendoza, we arranged to be among five passengers in a private station wagon that would climb to the pass, view *Christ of the Andes*, and descend the mountain into Santiago, the capital of Chile.

Halfway up the mountain, a tire blew. Ken and other passengers helped the driver change it. Luckily, he had a spare. The driver used the time to drink cha matte tea from an artistically carved gourd cup with a crafted sterling silver lip. A long handled silver spoon was the tea filter and served also as a straw through which the Matte was sipped. With the tire replaced, we proceeded to the pass. Climbing out of the car at the summit, we viewed the statue. In the distance was Mt. Aconcagua. Standing at the mountain pass between two countries felt exhilarating. If I had wings, I think this would be a launch pad. Ken spoke of returning to this area to do serious climbing. We began our descent into Santiago.

We lodged at a modest hostel and walked past the Presidential Palace on our way to the Planned Parenthood conference. Ken and I met doctors Alan Guttmacher and Mary Calderone and other world leaders in family planning. I was inspired by their leadership, professionalism, and compassion for women worldwide needing reproductive services.

21. Journey to the Sea: Voice of the River

I AM THE RIVER

Travel with me on my journey from mist to sea. I will meander, flow, and push my way across the continent. With heavy rain, I become angry and overflow my banks. Hear my story.

My birth begins as drops of rain high in the mountains of Venezuela. Other drops fall by my side, join with me to trickle over the rocks, uniting for the start of our adventure.

As flow gathers volume, I meander thousands of miles through primitive forests, along grazing fields, and by tiny villages where indigenous inhabitants tie their dugout canoes to posts. I am given a name, "Rio Salgado."

In the headwaters, I leave cousins who travel east and join relatives to contribute to the mighty Amazon and harbor the manatees at Manaus. I diverge from these cousins to discover the continent—heading east and south, flowing into northern Brazil, through the cacao region in southern Bahia, and on east to the port city of Ilhéus. My journey will end when I am old and tired. It is then that I will release all I hold and surrender to the mighty Atlantic.

As I flow, I listen to dialects. Native tongues like those spoken by the Kayapo, the Yanomami, and the Tupi-Guarani, are common deep within the rain forest. As I journey across the continent, I pass through colonies of Japanese, German, Syrian, and Lebanese and, closer to the ocean, mixed race African Brazilians and European descendants who speak Portuguese.

Fish and animals, inhabitants of my waters, have their own languages which I understand because I am multilingual, above and below the waters.

My waters caress and cradle. I take care of a variety of good eating fish, and a multitude of beautiful small fish. The anacondas are powerful rulers of the waters. The piranhas are the quick clean-up crew that leaves my waters clear of dying carcasses and debris. Inhabitants of my waters provide thousands of meals to poor and rich alike. Red, orange, yellow, and purple tropicals leave my waters to become pets in fish tanks in faraway countries.

Without questioning the politics, I travel by vast fields made by clear cutting the primeval forests. Silently, I provide water needed by the grazing cattle now occupying these fields. I flow in all seasons, mostly slow and deliberate, but at other times, fast and with anger. I hug the shores of villages whose people build homes close to me. One of those villages is Ibicaraí.

I make five sensual curves through this town, which slow and calm my waters. A stone and log bridge passes over me, connecting this quiet town to the lands and farms deeper in the stubby backlands. Outcroppings of boulders provide gathering places for villagers. On warm summer afternoons, I ease around my curves, tickle the feet of children, caress the arms of women who dip the family dishes into my waters, and hug the bodies of dogs who come to drink.

I listen as laundry women, bending close to do their work, speak softly and exchange family secrets. I enjoy the happy chatter as they rub clothes against the rocks and drape them to dry in the sun. When dried, the garments are neatly folded, placed into tall round reed baskets, and cushioned with a rolled-up cloth, the baskets are balanced on their heads. Swaying with their baskets, the women seem to be dancing the samba as they exit the river edge. I enjoy these ladies' presence and miss them as the dance away from my banks.

A tiny organism, a devious blood fluke that reproduces in my warm calm waters, is the Schistosoma. If I were to become angry, I would dislodge the pest. In its life cycle in my waters, the Schistosoma penetrates human skin, travels in the human's bloodstream, and infects them with disease and sometimes death. I say nothing, but simply move along contributing to life and disease.

Several journeys ago as recorded by the cycles of the moon, I became furious, riled up, and contributed to local flooding that damaged the village.

The humans had just celebrated a holiday. A skinny man in a red suit drove the main street in an open jeep, throwing candy to the children. For two days, the heavens opened and dumped rain upon the village. The volume of my waters became engorged, and I flowed with a strength I had not known. I rushed through the town, ruining my sensuous curves.

I shoved high onto the banks and flooded homes built with sticks and packed with mud, causing them to sag and fall. My waters became contaminated with filth. I was belligerent and the people were afraid, retreating into school buildings for shelter.

With tremendous force, I broke the bridge, half of it falling into my rushing waters. Mules strapped with reed baskets carrying metal cans of fresh milk stood on the part that remained intact. Burros laden with burlap bags filled with cacao beans had to find another path to the weigh station. I was aware of my enhanced power and lashed forward.

I felt relief only when I reached the port city of Ilhéus, where I regurgitated trash and debris into the greater expanse of the sea's salt waters. The rhythm and regularity of the surf calmed me.

Content to be pulled into ocean currents, I knew I would rise with the wind, ride the clouds in movement across sea and earth, fall within the mountain mist and be born to journey once again.

I AM THE RIVER.

22. Racism

AS PEACE CORPS VOLUNTEERS, we represented our country, warts included. We responded to questions of racism and politics in America. Friends and neighbors would ask. "Why is it you have such disparity among the races? Why are you so black and white? In Brazil we accept who we are and do not have separation. We are blended to many colors."

I think Brazil's racism is a gradual spectrum that goes from black to white with shades and tones in between. Names describe various shades. Preto, Moreno, mulatto, to Blanco—black to white. When one looks at the structure of the Brazilian society, those with lighter skin tend to hold leadership positions most frequently. Those of darker skin may be most laborers. This aligns with education and living opportunities. I think this mirrors our racism in the United States. Each country describes the other but fails to see racism in themselves. I am reminded of the different names I was given, such as "Dona Barbara," and "Dona Americana," and "Dona *Blanca*" (Mrs. White). My favorite name was affectionately, *Mia Negrainha* (My Little Negra). Whatever my name, I was addressed respectfully.

As mentioned earlier, both Martin Luther King, Jr. and Robert Kennedy were killed during our tour of duty in Brazil. These tragedies sparked discussions on race, guns, violence, politics, class, and color. One day, while traveling west, further into the interior of the state of Bahia, we visited a small town. I encountered a casually dressed elder sitting in the town square and introduced myself. He spoke with sadness, "I am so sorry about that young man."

Here, on a dusty street an elder, dressed in a short-sleeved shirt, worn khaki shorts, and flip flops, offered me condolences for the death of Robert Kennedy. How did he even know? Why would he care to give me comfort when I was a stranger and far from my home in America? The name Kennedy was revered and hopeful to the world, and this elder gave me his sympathy across cultures and language barriers. I felt deeply his compassion, love, and understanding of loss from one human comforting another.

It has been fifty-five years since my encounter with the elder and the assassinations of MLK, Jr. and Kennedy; two years since the murder of George Floyd documented on a cell phone video; one hundred years since the massacre of 300 people and destruction of an entire prosperous Black community, "Black Wall Street," in Oklahoma. For many, our collective sense of social justice has not moved forward from the days in 1691 when slave ships brought Africans to the Americans to build the economics on which the new country thrived. The word "freedom" in the United States is envisioned from various perspectives of where one is in the caste system. As a society, we are beginning to examine the meaning and practice of "institutionalized racism."

Reflection 2021: For Mother's Day this year, my daughter gave me a recently published book, The Three Mothers, by Anna Malaika Tubbs, a story of the mothers of Martin Luther King, Jr., Malcolm X, and James Baldwin. The years of their mothering were against the background of Jim Crow, lynching of black men and women, harassment, destruction and death by the Ku Klux Klan, denial of educational opportunities, and relegation to menial jobs, if hired at all. How did these three Black women raise their sons to have an indelible impact on our nation? Malcolm's mother Louise Little taught her children about their activist roots. Berdis Baldwin encouraged James to express himself through writing. Alberta King centered her teaching in lessons in faith and social justice. All three mothers taught their sons that every human being deserved dignity and respect and to stand tall in the confrontation with discrimination.

23. Farewell to Friends

1968

FOR OVER TWO YEARS, Ken and I lived at the edge of town, between the busy central hub with its hand-built, cobbled stone streets and a long stretch of a hard-packed clay road that extended to the main asphalt highway connecting with neighboring towns. Along our road were modest homes of the laundry women and laborers of the *fazendas*, rural farms in the campo. Roads connected the *barrios* and radiated from the town hub like spider legs.

Ken and I had been welcomed into this community, listened to the concerns, expressed our opinions, and built plans together for a stronger, more inclusive community. Living among common folk, speaking their language, devouring warm bread from the bakery, or a *cafezinho* with neighbors, our lives were forever enriched. A friend once asked me back in the States if I had feared for my safety or was threatened in any way. The simple answer was "No." But I have one regret.

Standing at my back door one night, in the quiet of darkness, I could hear chanting, singing, and drumming coming through the night calm—mesmerizing and inviting. I wanted to walk toward the sound, be welcomed into it, and allow myself to become absorbed by its trance-like effect. I stood still, listened, and didn't step forward, fearful I would be drawn into a trance from which I would not want to return. I, who likes to walk into the unknown to know, held back. I remained safely where I stood, framed in the back door of my home, looking out into the dark night. In section IV and under the tutelage of novelist Jim Lynch, I addressed this regret with a fictional rendition.

When the Salgado River overflowed its banks in what the news reports recorded as the "twenty-year flood," I saw the towns people come together. Ken and I had been entertaining a small group of Peace Corps Volunteers who had congregated at our house for the holiday. After a lovely Brazilian dinner, most of the Volunteers returned to their assigned towns. Ed remained to visit. The rains began. As the river crept up its banks, the mud-built homes took on water and collapsed. The water man with his burro and cart carrying large casks of well water began delivering to those in need. Ed joined us in helping the local priest and the *Prefeito* (mayor) assess the damage. The state department of health asked me to conduct a survey of needs to which I added a few questions on family planning.

A letter home to our parents concerning flood damage resulted in the generosity of the Presbyterian Church in Dayton taking a special collection and sending a sizable check. The town leadership and priest used the money to build a new home for a widow and her young son. It was a good start to rebuilding.

I wrote to the Director of *Servico Especial de Saude Publico (SESP)*, the Brazilian public health agency in Rio de Janeiro, asking for an appointment. My intention was to inform the federal administration of the status of health care at the clinic and to request a Brazilian trained Registered Nurse to replace me. To prepare for travel and my appearance for the meeting, my neighbor sewed a tailored yellow linen suit in the style of a successful businesswoman. Before I met with the Director of Brazil Public Health or *SESP*, I reviewed my remarks with the Director of U.S. Peace Corps Brazil. This was the first time a volunteer would meet with the head of Brazil's national health agency. Not only was the Director of *SESP* present but also three of his top aides. Speaking in my best Portuguese, I gave a report of the health needs in the interior, away from city centers. I returned to my town and heard soon after that a trained public health registered nurse would be assigned to replace me and carry on the work I had begun.

Guests for our final farewell celebration dinner were Jací, Netinha, Altamira, who occupied our back bedroom since the flood, and Luiz. Our packed handmade leather trunks were picked up retrieved, taken to Salvador, and shipped to our home in Ohio. Jací's parents gave us a farewell gift of a live chicken. Altamira cut its throat and drained the blood into a pan. After congealing to a solid consistency, it was chopped, sauteed with garlic, onion, peppers, and spices for the delicacy sarapatel, a dish you could best enjoy by not knowing its origin. Side dishes of rice, tomatoes, mango, and papaya accompanied the roast chicken entree. Plantains were sliced and fried in butter, sugar, and cinnamon. Coffee with milk completed the meal. The friendships made in this town were treasures and gave a focus to our path home, guiding us further into community service.

The white house with the blue door was my beloved sense of place. It held treasured memories—living among friends, listening to their stories, speaking their language, and drinking cafēzinho in small cups in their homes made of mud waddle.

Upon return to the United States, Ken and I applied our experience in inner city community development work. Ken worked for the City of Cincinnati as a planner for equity in neighborhood housing. He was a volunteer with the Association for the Blind, taking members on hikes and field trips. Ken, near the end of his life and sober for over forty years, counseled those with alcohol addiction. I worked in public health – organizing immunization clinics in Houston in response to a measles outbreak, developed access to maternal and child health care for indigent women in Washington state, and worked with a small tribe of indigenous women for equal access to health care. Our friendships and work within a diverse community in Brazil continues to enrich our lives.

24. Homeward Bound: Tour of Duty Complete

1968

OUR GROUP OF PEACE CORPS VOLUNTEERS had been in Brazil over two years—teaching, nursing, constructing, organizing, performing whatever tasks were asked of us. We questioned the U.S. State Department representative at our final debriefing, before we disbanded to travel to our homes in the States, how we would know if we had made a difference. The state department rep responded without hesitation: "You may never know the impact you have had, but twenty years from now, one person in the town where you served, one person you taught, or one person with whom you worked, votes in an election that makes a difference. You can leave your assignment knowing that you have done your best to create positive change."

Volunteers were given flight tickets home or the equivalent in cash. Ken and I took the cash. Our trip home would not be a direct flight from Brazil to Ohio, but rather a trek on a tight budget across the South American continent, traveling in a northerly direction. Dressed in tropical travel clothes and carrying small bags, we began. We hoped to be in Dayton by Christmas. We had six weeks.

From Rio, we took a coach through the German beer capital in Rio Grande do Sul and visited Iguazu Falls on the borders of Brazil, Argentina, and Paraguay. We boarded a train north to Asuncion, the capital of Paraguay. Planning to take a river boat north through Paraguay, we would have to wait four days for the boat. With the absence of seasonal rainfall, the river did not support river traffic, so instead of waiting a day longer, we cruised south on a flat-bottom boat and crossed the border into northern Argentina. We stepped off the boat at the town of Formosa and onto a train heading west, across the Grand Pampas to Embarcación, just south of the Bolivian border. So slow was the train that the flies continued to buzz around the lights to annoy us.

The train came to a stop in the barren pampas. I looked out the window for a station and saw nothing. One man dressed as a Gaucho—wearing baggy brown pants appropriate for riding; a blousy long sleeve shirt, cuffed at the wrist; a bright red neck scarf wrapped jauntily, tall leather boots and floppy brimmed hat—descended the steps and with a confident stride, walked in the direction of the setting sun. He became a silhouette at dusk. As the train began its slow pace forward, I watched the man, alone, step into the horizon. I would hold the romance of that picture forever.

We disembarked on the Argentine side at Embarcación and walked a mile north across the border into Bolivia and climbed aboard a train for Cochabamba. The night was chilly, and the native people noticed our tropical-weight clothing, not adequate for the night mountain air. They wrapped us in blankets, which we wore like ponchos, and gave us bags of candy to hide inside the blankets. We sat side by side, four people to a bench, facing four people on the opposite bench. Our sixteen knees touched in the center. Children sat at our feet. Not long into the ride, the guard made his rounds. He assessed the scene, spoke harshly to me, and demanded to know who gave me the blankets. I heard his question, but shrugged my shoulders, indicating I did not understand his language. He spoke louder. I again shrugged. He gave up trying. I suppose it had something to do with border taxes. The candy and blankets travelled through, and I slept snug in the night. By morning light, I could see llama herds on the Bolivian high plateau, attended by a shepherd dressed in a poncho and bowler hat. (A shepherd guards his sheep. What is the name of the guardian of llamas? A *llamaherd?*)

The train made a brief stop at an archaeological site, where the government was uncovering ancient Andean artifacts. No one was on site, and the ruins were open to vandalism and theft. Was the government too poor to have security for the ruins? From a vendor, we purchased two twelve-inch stone carvings that looked like aliens from space carrying backpacks. Not only did these carvings add weight to our limited luggage, but I wondered if they were indeed replicas of found artifacts and not the artifacts themselves stolen from an archeological site?

From Cochabamba, the beautiful city of flowers, we flew to La Paz, a city in the mountains where the airport is at a higher elevation than the capital city. The streets were steep. I remember climbing halfway up a street and feeling so tired I had to sit down in the center of the sidewalk. Ken, energized by the mountain air, continued to the top and waited while I regained my oomph to continue climbing. It was about this time that I had an inkling that my fatigue was because I had conceived, as I had discontinued using birth control when we left Rio.

A hefty tin ore boat stood at the dock, waiting for eight passengers to board and accompany the freight across Lake Titicaca to Puno, Peru. We were invited aboard. Ken and I joined six other passengers, reached for the handrail, and stepped aboard. Deep, large, freshwater Lake Titicaca is the highest navigable lake in the world. Its elevation above sea level is 12,507 feet. By volume of water and by surface area, it is the largest lake in South America. Its surface area is 3,232 square miles. I am cruising on a commercial tin ore boat high in the Andes crossing the border from Bolivia to Peru.

The passengers dined with the captain. Seated with us were two Chilean women, a British theologian and his wife, and a Bolivian couple on holiday. At dawn the next morning, equipped with binoculars, I joined the British theologian on deck. I had heard native families lived on reed islands in the lake, and we hoped to see fishermen in reed canoes. We strained to see but were unable to glimpse movement through the mist. We accepted, however, the fresh morning breeze on our cheeks as we listened to the rhythm of the bow separating the water toward Puno. Below the freighter, in the depths of the water, were ancient civilizations made famous by the diving films of Jacque Cousteau. Looking into the water, I imagined that I was a SCUBA diver of the Cousteau team exploring an ancient civilization, visualizing the reed homes I had once seen on a TV documentary.

Docking at Puno, we boarded a train for Cusco and enjoyed seeing the countryside, rural homes, and farm animals walking free, unencumbered by fences. Arriving at Cusco, we arranged lodging at a hostel in the central plaza across the park from the magnificent Basilica Cathedral of the Assumption of Cusco, a Spanish Colonial monument.

Travelling third class on a five-hour train ride with the local native people, our train switchedbacked the hairpin curves up the mountain out of Cusco toward Machu Picchu. By word-of-mouth, we learned that one ancient ruin had been thatched so that budget travelers like us could sleep the night. To prepare for our trip up the mountain, I attended morning market. From the weaver sitting at her loom, I purchased two thick wool blankets. From a vendor under her canopy, I purchased fruit, wine, and cheese. Joining us for the trip to the site was another Peace Corps couple, Bob and Mary Ann, who had completed their assignment in Bolivia and were heading home to Montana. Another non-native was on the train, a student from Israel named Abraham. Native mountain villagers filled the rest of the seats.

Within the canyon along the Urubamba River and far below Machu Picchu, the train stopped, and we were met by a van driver to shuttle us to the top of the mountain. I remember looking up. I could not see Machu Picchu from below; there was no evidence that a civilization had once existed here. Riding up a narrow switchbacked gravel road, we reached the sacred site. A small lodge was available for tourists, but the five of us— Bob, Mary Ann, Abraham, Ken, and I stowed our backpacks in the only ruin that had a thatched roof and straw strewn on the cold stone floor. We stepped out to tour.

Stone-walled agricultural terraces wound horizontally across the surface of the mountain, like giant stair steps eight feet in height and the same in width. The Incas who lived here at the time of the Spanish conquest of Peru grew their potatoes and vegetables on these terraces, complete with an irrigation system that began at the top level. We walked in and out of the remains of buildings that once were the homes and workshops of the city's residents. Stone pathways, carefully placed, linked homes, storerooms, and temple. As my feet touched the walkway, I felt the stones sharing the stories of life under the clouds. I listened. In the silence, I heard the wind whispering as if music accompanied my walk. I stood at the altar in the temple and looked through its three windows, which opened to the Urubamba River canyon and toward the sun. It is from this sacred space that the summer solstice is honored. This temple was constructed facing the sun as were the Mayan Temples of Chichén Itzá in the Yucatán, the Egyptian Pyramids along the Nile, Stonehenge in England, and Serpent Mound in Lucas County, Ohio—all in perfect alignment for celebration of the Solstice, "the day when the sun appears to reach its most northerly or southerly excursion relative to the celestial equator on the celestial sphere" (Wikipedia).

Accompanied by the dog that lived at the lodge, Mary Ann and Bob, Ken and I climbed Una Pichu, the sentry location above Machu Picchu. From this vantage summit, we could see the layout of the entire village of Machu Picchu, look down upon the Urubamba River, and see movement in the valley below. Yet, from below, as I remembered upon arriving looking up at Machu Picchu, we could see only the stones on the mountain surface. As the daughter of an Ohio farm girl, annually and intuitively planting my backyard garden vegetables, I felt kin to the ancient farmers who planted potatoes on these agricultural terraces, which in a horizontal and parallel pattern, graced the mountain side.

As night was falling at our site at the top of the mountain under the clouds, we retreated to our stone hutch. The five of us gave each other human warmth. We broke bread, poured wine, ate cheese, and spoke of our travels to this sacred place. Wrapped in wool blankets, we set our heads to rest on the floor feeling connection with the ancient villagers who once slept here and who toiled these terraces. I believe their spirits guarded our rest through the night.

Inspired and satisfied that we had slept the night in a sacred space, we returned by train to Cuzco. If we curtailed additional travel across South America, we could be home by Christmas. We flew to Lima. Booking a ticket on a prop jet, we flew to Quito, Ecuador, then on to Panama City and Miami, Florida. We hustled through United States Customs and onto a full flight, flying from Miami to Seattle to debrief with my sister and her family before heading home to parents in Ohio. Still in our tropical travel clothing, my sister met our flight with coats, scarves, and gloves. It was snowing in Seattle. After getting the feel of re-entering American culture, we flew to Dayton for Christmas.

The question we Peace Corps volunteers asked the U.S. State Department representative in Rio has remained central to our continued work at home. The opportunity to serve a community different from the communities in which we had been born, to speak a language not English, to live within the creativity of community diversity, forever enriched, informed, and changed our lives. The difference was within us.

25. Birthing

1969, 1972

ABOUT THE TIME NEIL ARMSTRONG AND BUZZ ALDRIN were returning from the moon, I went into labor. Ken drove the VW bug, giving me verbal encouragement while checking the clock. We drove in circles until the clock struck midnight, then headed to the hospital, wanting to save the cost of an extra day's stay. I breathed through contractions as we drove closer to the Emergency Room. These were the days before childbirth classes and fathers allowed in the delivery room. My obstetrician was a friend of my parents and a member of the Presbyterian Church, so I trusted him to keep me safe. I remember Dr. Barr wanted me to keep my pregnancy weight to fourteen pounds. Today, that seems out-of-date and unhealthy.

Our first daughter Suellen, named for her aunts, was born in the early morning, exiting at seven pounds plus. The doctors kept her under the lights, as they said she appeared jaundiced. Celebrating her birth, the newborn received visitors: my mother, Ken's mother and father, my great Aunt Cal, and Presbyterian ministers of two congregations, all came to bestow blessings. With great joy, Suellen was welcomed into the community.

At the time of Suellen's birth, Ken and I lived on Dayton West Side, a Black neighborhood, halfway between my mother on the northside and Ken's parents on the south. The astronauts were safely returned to earth and released from quarantine. Suellen thrived. When she was six weeks old, we moved to Cincinnati and rented the first floor of a home, just four houses from the university campus. Ken entered the Community

Development master's program, and I was a night private duty nurse at Jewish Hospital. I was able to nurse my baby before leaving for work at night and again in the morning when I returned. She cooperated in this teamwork by sleeping while I was on duty. I quit private duty when my obese arrogant cataract patient made a sexual comment about my full breasts. I felt that I was mostly babysitting him anyway, while down the hall was an indigent patient who could have benefitted from private duty care. I was aware of the inequities, how the wealthy could buy into our healthcare system, and I did not like what I was experiencing. I went to work for Planned Parenthood.

The next school year, I entered the University of Cincinnati master program for Health Planning. Trudy Karlson, a fellow student with the same health planning focus became my partner for a thesis project, and together we set up a Women's Health Care clinic within the student health service. Trudy and I taught from the Boston Women's Health Collective's publication, Our Bodies, Ourselves. I worked with Planned Parenthood to promote women's access to health care, honoring their commitment to offer non-discriminatory health care service to all. When the university announced the appointment of a new President who was the guru of Planning Change, Dr. Warren Bennis, several planning students joined Ken and me in driving to Buffalo to meet Dr. Bennis before his move to Cincinnati. In Dr. Bennis's home, the student group discussed the planning of change. One afternoon, after Dr. Bennis took his position in Cincinnati, he walked across campus to our student apartment to meet with students.

Ken and I began planning the birth of our second child. Everything was in order and to our delight, second daughter was born as the country celebrated its birthday, July 4, 1972. Named Audrey Elizabeth, after her grandmother and royalty. This was a time of change in obstetrical services, and Christ Hospital, where I delivered, was instituting a program called "rooming in," meaning the baby could stay in the room with the mother, although extended family members could not visit. When Ken's parents drove down from Dayton to see the new grandchild, the hospital would not allow visitation. To have the baby's grandparents drive an hour to see their new grandchild and return home without seeing her, was not okay. Not knowing how to buck the system, I did not speak up and demand visiting rights. I sank into postpartum depression and sobbed for hours. The nursery nurse came to take care of my baby, and the postpartum nurse came to sit with me. The hospital protocol would not budge. I cried for as long as I had the energy to do so. It was postpartum depression.

26. Drinking

I DID NOT COME FROM A DRINKING FAMILY. Outside of the whiskey toddy located on the top shelf in the kitchen, kept for Grandpa when he was ailing, I did not know what a bottle of booze looked like. Until college…

Ken had been a fraternity man, a handsome one with close-cropped hair and a husky, sexy voice. He drank, smoked, and had a gregarious, magnetic personality. I became the fraternity princess. Drinking was a part of the weekend party scene. Ken's parents relaxed with a pleasant daily happy hour, and I gave little thought to the pattern of at-home drinking. In graduate school, students came to our apartment with a large bottle of Chianti, and we discussed planning change. My strategy was if I shared the bottle of wine, there would be less wine for Ken to drink, but it did not work that way. An empty wine bottle was replaced with another.

When Ken could not get up after a night of drinking, I was disappointed, ticked off. Yet, I did not speak by directly confronting the problem. To cope, I channeled my anger into cleaning the apartment. Once the apartment was neat and clean, my anger dissipated. Meanwhile, Suellen grew from an infant into a three-year-old. Once, when I felt I could not cope, I sat on the edge of our bed and cried. Suellen climbed up on the bed and put her arms around me to provide comfort. Too much responsibility for a three-year-old.

One night, I attended an Al Anon meeting, a support group for family members of alcoholics. The group cordially welcomed me, but I felt confused, awkward, and uncomfortable. I left the meeting and never returned. Ken was upset with me for going. I withdrew into myself, not sharing my hurt with friends. There were times when I ran out of the apartment and walked the streets. One night it was quite cold, and I had not taken time to grab a coat. I walked until I felt frozen and needed warmth. Ken was relieved to have me return.

I remember one night, not long after Audrey's birth, Ken left the house to go to a bar. On his way home, a block from our house, he drove into a tree, totaling the car. The policeman who came to take the report wrote up a ticket for "changing lanes," evading a more serious drinking charge. It seemed to me the patrolman let him off, and Ken could once again evade consequences of his drinking. This recalls another piece of the puzzle that I had not thought of until the "changing lanes citation."

Ten years before this incident when we were volunteers in Brazil, the cheap local cachaça was Ken's drink of choice. It was rum made from sugar cane and the local variety was not so refined as the bestselling brands. With the cachaça lubricating their voices, Ken joined the troubadours, a group of night rovers. One of our fellow Peace Corps volunteers, concerned about Ken's drinking expressed concern to the Peace Corps doctor. Ken was escorted from our assigned town to a psychiatric hospital outside Washington, D.C.

I traveled to the state capital, Salvador, to await word of Ken's treatment. It was possible Ken would not return to Brazil and both of us would be asked to leave our assignment. A group of sympathetic volunteers who had assignments in towns strewn across the southern state of Bahia organized to bring Ken back to Brazil to complete his literacy project.

We needed more information and wanted to talk directly to Ken concerning his health status. I heard of a ham operator who lived in a distant barro in Salvador, so we boarded the local bus to see him. A jolly robust man opened the door and led us to his second-floor communication studio, which consisted of a large switchboard, antennas, and headphones. It was an impressive command center.

"Ken is an inpatient on the ward at Brooks Psychiatric Hospital in Washington, D.C." we told the ham operator. Focusing on location, he connected with a peer in North America, who patched the call through to the hospital in Washington, D.C. and to the ward where Ken resided. Ken answered the phone. We cheered!

"Ken, how are you?"

"I am fine, healthy, and ready to return to work."

"That's what we wanted to hear! Across continents, it's amazing to hear you so clearly. We hope to see you soon, back in Brazil, on the job." The volunteers felt victorious in this cross-equator connection.

When Ken and I returned to our assigned town, we avoided confronting the issue—drinking that necessitated evacuation, need for in-patient psychiatric treatment, and pretending it was just a bit of social drinking with the street people. We avoided looking deeper into the root causes, preferring to skirt the issue, saying, "Ken is a social drinker…"

Five years after returning from Peace Corps service and home to the States and with two growing daughters, Ken's drinking continued and began to affect family relations. Ken and I went to Family Services for marriage counseling. We also attended two separate peer-groups, groups that were a mixture of men and women, alcoholics, and spouses of alcoholics. I believe we gave it our best effort, but ultimately, we failed to keep the marriage together....

It has been forty-six years ago; Ken and I were divorced in a simple court action called dissolution. Our marriage of ten years, packed with the adventures of Peace Corps volunteer service and the birth of two daughters, was dissolved. Both of us loved the girls and put our focus on their needs in growth and education. I remarried and birthed a daughter. Ken remarried and his wife, also a nurse, birthed a daughter. Between the two of us, we have four daughters. We hike together when there is a family reunion. The two daughters who are not half-sisters to each other, call themselves "quarter" sisters.

On one of my return visits to Cincinnati, visiting after I was well established in the Pacific Northwest, Ken asked me to accompany him to an AA meeting. I met his friends, participated in the meeting, and came to understand how addiction to alcohol affects behavior, something I did not know years before. Over the years, Ken had become a mentor to many who struggled with alcohol addiction. Most importantly, he was devoted to the growth and education of his daughters and my good friend until his death.

Our honeymoon long ago at Mt. LeConte on the Appalachian Trail began Ken's lifetime goal to hike the entire Appalachian Trail from Springer, Georgia, to Mt. Katahdin in Maine, which he accomplished near the end of his life. When he was completing the last mile, his daughters, third wife, and sister joined him, celebrating the importance of this accomplishment. Ken died on October 31, 2017, unexpectedly, but "serenely," his wife said. His memorial was held in the undercroft of the Catholic Basilica of Cincinnati, the available space that could accommodate his many friends and family close to the Thanksgiving holiday. I wrote a eulogy that spoke to his legacy. I grieve the loss of a good man, my former husband, a man who maintained sobriety for forty years. I ponder—if I had known now what I had not known back then, what might have been?

27. The Politics of Portuguese Vocabulary

THESE PORTUGUESE WORDS are not just with dictionary definition, but statements of why these particular words were important living in a culture and speaking a language not our own.

Alfabetização: Literacy; teaching of reading; (*alfabeto*, alphabet). I believe that nothing can be more important for world peace than teaching a person to read and write. It leads to voting, participation in own's society.

Arroz: Rice. Accompanying the black beans, our daily meal. It was served in all homes whether rich or poor, *fazendeiro* (ranch owner) or *tralbalhador* (workman).

Banana de prata: Banana of the plate, the common banana as we know them. I shall never forget the vendor of bananas who positioned on his head a large basket of bananas and sang as he danced the samba and shuffled down the street, *"Bananas de prata, bananas de prata, bananas, bananas, bananas."*

Barro: In the Portuguese dictionary, this word means clay. It is also the word for neighborhood. Our work was in the *barros*, in the streets and in the homes of the community. *Barrio* in Spanish means neighborhood.

Cacau: Cocoa. A main economy of Southern Bahia. Processed into fine powder for chocolate and exported to world markets. From those markets, sweet chocolate bars returned, thus providing rich income to the middle market.

Cafezinho: A demitasse cup of thick syrupy black coffee, with added sugar. Even in the most modest of homes, visitors were always welcome, shown respect and offered a *cafezinho*.

Diarreia: Diarrhea, a health concern where sanitation is limited, and intestinal parasites prevalent. My earlier story tells of the sad loss of newborns to diarrhea and dehydration.

Empregada: Employed as a female maid within the household; *empregado*, hired man. Many rural people migrated into the cities; women becoming *empregadas* in the homes of the wealthy. During draught, people of the Northeast migrated to the south, often to industrial São Paulo to find work.

Feijão: Beans; *feijão prêto*, black beans which we ate daily. Daily! I might add, Ken and I managed to put on a bit of weight with this daily national dish.

Feijoada: Black bean stew, made with adding available meats and vegetables to the bean pot. It is the soul of Brazil and when I serve this dish for family or company or church auction, everyone claims it as their very own soul food. International known novelist Jorge Amado wrote an endearing tale of a beautiful *empregada* cook in *Gabriella, Clavo e Canela* (Gabriella, Clove and Cinnamon). This dish is the blending of culture: Native, African, and European spices. *Muito gostoso* (very savory, very delicious).

Farinha: Grainy flour with no nutritive value. I was concerned that this made up a part of the diet of the poor. I had hoped that research could substitute this filler for a more nutritious grain.

Farofa: Farinha sautéed in butter, onions, garlic, cilantro, and served over black beans and rice, adding a nutty texture to the dish.

Ginásio: High school. As mentioned in the story, ten young women with a *ginásio* education became the *professoras* for the literacy classes. When I returned to visit Ibicaraí twenty years after my assignment, one of the former *professoras* came up to me in the handsome new Mercedes bus terminal built after my departure. She asked, "Are you Dona Barbara?"

"Yes," I said.

"I always hoped you would return."

We hugged and cried, happy to be reunited and recognizing the importance of what the literacy program contributed to community development.

Hora de Abutre: Hour of the vulture, time of dusk, Ken's favorite time of the day when the vultures begin to circle. A special end-of-day ritual, reconvening neighborhood togetherness.

Passear: To take a walk, to promenade. A time for young people to see and be seen. When couples paired up, they were chaperoned, often by a younger sibling.

Rio de Janeiro: River of January. What an incredibly beautiful city. On top of Mount Corcovado, the outstretched arms of the statue of Christ welcomes, and from the height, one views lovely beaches, famous for bikini bathing suits. To get to the top of the hill, ride the cog rail train car which slowly cranks from street level to the Christ. When I visited, twenty years after my assignment, I took eight-year-old daughter Emily with me. We took the rail car up. When we arrive on top, Emily climbed aboard the car returning down. When I saw her enter, it was already too late for me; the door had closed. I followed her in the next car. When she got to the bottom, she took the next car to the top while I was going down. I spoke to the operators of my dilemma and with their help, waited at the bottom for her to take the next car down. I purchased a batik at the gift shop to commemorate this cog train adventure.

Salgado: Salted, witty; piquant. This was the name of the river that flowed through Ibicaraí. After hearing the voice of the river, you'll think the river was well named.

Sarapatel: Highly spiced giblet stew in which clotted blood is an ingredient. It is a tasty and nutritious dish, but I preferred not to know its ingredients.

Saúde: Health. My Registered Nurse license and training were needed to work in the federal health post where few trained nurses were available. *Saúde* is the toast given among friends as in "to your health."

Sertão: Scrubby prairie area, backlands well described in Jorge Amado's novels. At Maron's, a local bar in Ilhéus, the townspeople plus volunteers congregated to eat kibbeh and drink beer. Kibbeh is a Lebanese recipe of ground meat, onion, and spices such as allspice and ground cinnamon baked or deep fried as a croquette and celebrated in Amado's novels.

Brazilian Friends and Neighbors Featured in these Stories.

Altamira, A young woman who lived in our home after the floods. She was the one who killed and dressed (or undressed) the chickens I bought at market and prepared the chicken for our farewell dinner, also making *sarapatel*.

Dona Joanna, our landlady and next-door neighbor was the most respected midwife in town. I appreciated and honored the commitment and quality of her midwifery.

Dona Maria, our neighbor next door and Dona Joanna's housemate. She taught Ken to pound and grind coffee beans, and she taught me to prepare *feijoada*, a daily black bean stew, prepared over charcoal in a locally hand-crafted clay pot.

Jací, was my co-worker in public health and whom I mentored. She attended the state public health conference, the only attendee not from the coastal cities. She was tall, dark complexioned and walked with confidence. Her father was Portuguese and her mother Native Tupi-Guarani. I heard years after that Jací died in a traffic accident in Rio de Janeiro. Emily and I planted a cherry tree in our front yard to Jací's memory.

Luiz Barbosa Santos was the young man Ken mentored to be the organizer of the literacy program in Ibicaraí. When I visited in 1988, Luiz was working as a contractor and had moved his wife and two children to Ilhéus. Luiz was hired by Peace Corps and came to the States to teach a group of volunteers heading for assignment in Brazil. Over the years, I have lost contact and would like to renew correspondence with Luiz.

Netinha was our laundry woman and close friend who kept us informed of neighborhood events. She is pictured with her baby in our quintal.

When I visited with Emily, the beautiful baby was a lovely young woman of 20.

Jorge Amado. Born August 10, 1912 on a hacienda near Itabuna, a neighboring city of Ibicaraí, Jorge Leal Amado de Faria earned international acclaim for his novels of the people of southern Bahia. He is one of the most famous of Brazilian writers. His books were translated into 47 languages. My two favorites were *Dona Flor e Seus Dois Maridos*, (Dona Flor and Her Two Husbands) and Gabriela, Cravo e Canela, (Gabriela, Clove and Cinnamon.) Ken and I ate at a bar in Ilhéus made famous in his writings.

28. Photographs – Ken and Barbara

Under the Tiffany Te Deum-stained glass window, Ken and I were married in the Westminster Presbyterian Church, Dayton, Ohio, August 28, 1965.

Passport photo. Ken and I were invited into the United States Peace Corps in the spring of 1966 for Community Development work in the state of Bahia, Brazil. I had my official Passport photo stamped into the blue folder. As a public health nurse, I was ready to work in a rural small-town clinic on the edge of the *sertão*.

This was our home in Ibicaraí. The federal public health worker is spraying the bottom of the chairs and tables with DDT as a preventative measure against malaria and Chagas Disease carried by mosquito. 1966.

The cobblestone pavement was laid by hand. This is a typical street on which we lived. Homes were built one story only and close together. Many of the streets in outlying areas were not paved, but of hard packed clay. Transportation of horse and cart was common. I remember visiting further into the interior of the state where one vender came to Saturday market in ox cart with wooden wheels that turned on a wooden axle. The rotation of the wheel groaned as in a movie of the dark ages.

Saturday Market brought the townspeople and those who lived in the compo together to exchange news and buy the necessities for the week. The lady in the top picture crafted my clay bean pot and carved my stirring spoon. Since we had no refrigeration, Saturday market replenished my supply of eggs, vegetables, fruits, and milk brought to market in large metal cans on the backs of mules. We knew to boil the milk for protection from bovine tuberculosis.

Altamira examines the beans. She will scoop them into a muslin bag with the name of *feizão* stitched onto the front to identify the contents. Black beans and rice called Feijoada is the national dish of Brazil, and I purchased the black beans at Saturday Market. Altamira would also help me buy chicken by selecting the plumpest and then kill and prepare for cooking, draining the blood for the delicacy sarapatel.

My neighbor and friend, Déte, washed her family's clothes in the river. At the time, the river was contaminated with schisto-somiasis, a liver fluke that penetrated the skin and caused illness. We treated the illness in the clinic and encouraged the town to build a central well water system.

Luis Barbosa Santos, center, was the organizer of the cross-town literacy program which working folks attended in the evening. Laundry women who had washed their clients' clothes in the river, and men who cut the cacao fruit pods from the trees in the cacao grove, came freshly attired to learn to read. When they could sign their name, they could vote. Luis' brother, Esmeraldo, is pictured at right. Person to left is unknown. Ken was Luis' mentor using Paulo Freire's curriculum, *Pedagogy of the Oppressed*.

Netinha, our laundry woman, and her baby are pictured in our backyard garden. When I said, "Netinha, you can't enter the contaminated river to wash my clothes," she responded, "Then, I will wash the clothes of another. It is the way I make my living." Ken and I worked to engage the entire town from Prefeito (mayor), town council, and health post personnel to working folks in a campaign to build a central water system.

This gentleman was our postmaster. Our mail always came through without problems; it was good to hear from family back home. He was also the leather trunk maker and helped us ship home our treasured art in three of these strong wood trunks with metal corners and latches. The bicycles were ours for riding around town.

The children love to suck on the sugar cane. They need only to peel away the outer skin to access the sweet fibers beneath. The cane is pressed to release the sugar juice. Work in the sugar cane fields prompted the slave masters to enslave those from West Africa and transport them across the Atlantic to the Brazilian coast. If adults have missing front teeth, you might guess that they sucked sugar cane and did not have proper dental care to counteract the damage.

I successfully advocated for a Public Health Nurse assigned by SESP, the federal public health agency, to replace me in Ibicaraí. The community would continue to be served by an R.N. when Ken and I completed our service. A twenty-year flood damaged homes along the river. Residents took temporary refuge in school buildings, and I became a visiting public health nurse. The Italian nuns equipped me with over-the-counter medicines sent by Catholic Charities. The Presbyterian church back in Ohio took up a collection. Our assistance to flood victims became a global effort.

An authentic feijoada, the national dish of Brazil is pictured against the cobblestone streets of a Brazilian town, Ouro Prêto. The principal components of a feijoada are (clockwise): black beans in the chafing dish, collards, farina, meats, onion rings, oranges, roast pork and rice.

Craig Claiborne in the New York Times Cookbook clearly describes the ingredients of the *Feijoada Completa.* I prepare this meal for family gatherings or donate as a dinner at the annual church action or a fundraiser for United Way and the Nurses Association. It is a hit in any culture and in any time. When I took my young daughter with me for a return to Brazil, we visited Ouro Prêto and ate at the restaurant on the left side of the street where a man is now standing. This is a colonial town, the first capital of Brazil, located in the state of Minas Gerais.

These eight-inch-tall stone figures were purchased at an excavation site on the Bolivian Highlands. They represent man and woman. We were travelling by train from Embarcación, Argentina to Cochabamba, Bolivia when we stopped to visit the ruins. The same figures are wearing backpacks making them interesting archeological studies.

Ken and I attend the International Planned Parenthood Conference in Santiago, Chile, 1967

The ancient Inca walls of Cuzco, Peru were so well constructed that the rocks fit together as a puzzle piece, no mortar needed. The Spanish constructed their temples over Inca walls. When there was an earthquake, the Spanish construction fell. The Inca wall stood firm.

Peruvian women were weaving blankets on our hike to ancient ruins above Cuzco. Children accompany their mother to the workplace. I purchased two blankets to sleep over in the ruins at Macho Picchu.

In November 1968, one of the Inca Macho Picchu ruins had a thatched roof with straw on the floor. Besides the two-hand woven wool blankets, I purchased wine, cheese, and bread at the market for our sleepover in the ruins. We accessed the mountain via a third-class Indian train, which switchbacked over the mountains and along the river.

Steep agricultural terraces sustained the population of the city. Spanish Conquistadores traveling in the valley below knew of such a city but never found it. The rocks blend the city into the environment. Macho Picchu was not discovered until it was long in ruins and covered with mountain growth.

Travel Across South American Continent
1967. Attend International Planned Parenthood Conference in Santiago, Chile
1. Ibicaraí, our Peace Corps assignment in cacão region of southern Bahia, Brazil.
2. South by bus to Rio de Janerio, São Paulo, Porto Alegre, to
3. Montevideo, Uruguay. Hydrofoil across bay to
4. Buenos Aires. Train west to Mendoza, wine region, foothills of the Andes.
5. With driver up narrow road, cross Andes in station wagon; pause at summit to view *Christ of the Andes*, descend mountain to Santiago.
6. Attend International Planned Parenthood Conference. Meet Edwardo Frei Montalva, Christian Democrat President of Chile. Meet world leaders in Family Planning, Agriculture, Literacy.
7. Return to Ibicaraí same route.

1968: Journey home to Dayton, Ohio
1. Say "até logo"(until later) to friends in Ibicaraí, our home of over two years.
2. South to Rio de Janerio and Curitiba.
3. West to Foz de Iguassu (Iguazu Falls) at borders of Brazil, Argentina, Paraguay.
4. West to Asunción, Paraguay. Plans to boat north cancelled due to low water level.
5. Float south to Argentine border. Board train across Grand Chaco, Northern Argentina to Embarcación. Walk one mile to train station in southern Bolivia.
6. Wrapped in blankets shared by the native passengers in crowded third class, Ken and I take the night train through highlands of central Bolivia to Cochabamba.
7. Fly to La Paz. Airport located on a high plateau in the mountains.
8. Sail on tin ore boat across Lake Titicaca, on border of Peru and Bolivia. Altitude 12, 497 feet (3,809m), highest large lake in the world. Disembark Puno, Peru.
9. Train to Cuzco, Peru through rural countryside.
10. In the Cuzco market plaza, purchase two hand-loomed blankets woven by Native women, bread, wine, and cheese.
11. Board third class train with local village folk; travel switchbacks by Urubamba River to Machu Picchu. Overnight on bed of straw over ancient stone floor of thatched roof ruin. Tour the abandoned community. Hike to Una picchu, the high lookout over the city.
12. Return to Cuzco. Fly to Lima and begin flights home via Quito, Ecuador, Panama City, Panama, to Miami, Florida. Diagonal flight across the United States to Seattle; snowing, my sister meets us with warm coats. Acclimate to American culture. Fly home to Dayton for Christmas with our parents.

Upon returning from Peace Corps, we began our family and entered the University of Cincinnati for Graduate work in Community and Health Planning. Suellen was our first child who grew up with graduate student discussions in the living room.

29. Kenneth Bradley Bordwell. A Eulogy

February 1, 1942 – October 30, 2017

HIS NAME WAS KENNETH. Brazilian friends called him "Kennis" and "Kennegy."

Once upon a time, fifty-one years ago in a small town of Brazil, a United States Peace Corps couple arrived to work in a Community Development project. She went to work at the health post. He went to work in the streets, made friends with the common folk. He sang with the troubadours at night. He danced the samba at Carnival and Micareta, the festivals before and after the observance of lent. He hosted volunteers for Christmas dinner and after the river overflowed its banks, he rebuilt homes of the poor who lived along the swollen riverbanks.

Luis, a young man with a fifth-grade education came to him one day, "Help me teach my neighbors how to read." Together, he and Luis talked and planned; they initiated a literacy campaign. Luis scoured the town for teachers. Ten women having finished *ginasio*, an eighth-grade equivalent, stepped forward. City officials gave the new program space in public buildings. Paulo Freire, Brazilian Secretary of Education, believed in grass-roots empowerment. His book, *Pedagogy of the Oppressed*, became the guidebook for the campaign. Ten classes held at various locations throughout the town began Monday evening. Who came?

Laundry women who spent the day washing clothes in the river, drying the garments over boulders, pressing the fabrics with charcoal irons, and delivering the neatly folded clothes in baskets they carried on their heads, came. With machetes, men spent the day cutting cacao fruit, collecting the fruit in woven baskets on the backs of mules, driving the animals to market, then returning to their homes for fresh shirts. They came. With pride, these women, and these men at the end of their workday, filed into literacy classes.

Two years later, when the Peace Corps assignment was over and the couple gave their final report to a State Department representative they asked, "How will we know if our work had influence?"

The representative responded, "You may never know, but twenty years from now, a vote will be held, and decisions made that will have an impact for change. People will participate because you empowered them to have a voice."

In all the work done in those two years to help develop the community, none was more important than teaching Luis' neighbors—the laundry women and the men in the cacao groves to read and write.

Luis' mentor for organizing the literacy program was Kenneth. But the town folk could not pronounce "th" of his American name. Many called him Kennis. Others called him Kennegy, after the beloved American President.

Written and read by Barbara Mould Bordwell Young

November 22, 2017,

St. Peter in Chains Cathedral, Cincinnati, Ohio

III. Prince of Con

1976-1990

HE SEEMED TO APPEAR OUT OF THE CLOUDS, funny, handsome, smart, wealthy. If he were a churchgoing family man, could a single woman go wrong to fall in love?

30. Encounter

1976

I WAS REARED IN A HARMONIOUS HOME and Sundays were devoted to the Presbyterian Church where my father served as an Elder. Although my mother had earned her Master of Social Work at The Ohio State University in 1941, she was a stay-at-home mom who closely guided my development as well as that of my sister and brother. My parent's relationship was the picture of a functional, contented marriage. I knew nothing of domestic violence, not even the term.

I married my college sweetheart in 1965, a relationship that lasted ten years. The marriage was legally dissolved, without acrimony, which meant my former husband and I co-parented our two children—Suellen, age five, and Audrey, age two. Ken's drinking and my inability to confront him had gotten in the way of communication. I was unable to speak the pain I felt and, therefore, left a marriage that might have worked if I had known how to cope with alcoholism.

To find stability after the divorce, I sought refuge within the Methodist Church Divorced and Singles Group, wanting to learn how others coped with a broken marriage. I was pleased that the church recognized not all parishioners were white middle or upper-class families of four—two parents, a boy, and girl—with at least one parent employed. I was now one of the others—single, recently divorced, two daughters, employed as an administrative assistant to a city councilman, and needing help with childcare.

The members of the Divorced and Singles Group were alert and talkative and ranged in age from twenty-five to fifty. The church was in an upscale neighborhood, and the members of my group were well-dressed, though casual in open-collar shirts and pull-over sweaters. One man, in his late thirties, a geek, stood out. It was because he came to the meeting in a two-piece conservative suit, black Florsheim laced shoes, Brooks Brothers white shirt, and red paisley silk tie. His eye twitched slightly as he cocked his head to get a better focus on the group. His three-year-old son was in the playroom next to our meeting. It had only been a few months since my divorce, but I felt it was okay to be impressed. I was attracted to this man's sense of humor as he interjected quick, clever comments into group discussion.. The well-dressed man seemed a sage, an elite among common folk. He was also handsome and gregarious.

"Hi, I am Freddie McMurray."

"Hi. I am Barbara." This is often the way it begins, I thought. He appeared to be financially successful. When I heard that he had a Ph.D., I assumed he was well educated. Hadn't my mother emphasized the benefits of advanced education.

The church announced a family retreat to a military boy's camp near the ancient Miamisburg Mound. I felt drawn to the visual of a camp in the woods under a canopy of autumn. I added my daughters and my names to the list. Freddie signed up,too.

Camp was south of where my mother lived in Dayton.. I invited her to join us for dinner. At mealtime, Mother met Freddie and noticed how attentive I was to his comments. "Now, don't you rush him," she advised. Intimidated by her comment, I shrunk into silence.

At the camp, we bunked in dorm rooms with men on one side of the long hallway and women on the other. Food was served cafeteria style and tasty for camp food. Weather was sunny and sweater crisp. To visit the pumpkin patch, we formed carpools. The kids and I piled into the cushy back seat of Freddie's long, large Lincoln Continental, along with another of the dads who climbed in front. Freddie 's car appeared to have been through miles of close calls by the evidence of dents, scrapes, and scratches. The beat-up Lincoln did not fit the image of a wealthy businessman.

"Pick the biggest pumpkin you can find, and I will buy it for you," Freddie told my daughters.

The girls took the challenge. They laughed as they ran down the rows, picking this one and that one, each better, well maybe, than the last. After a thorough search, measuring each with their hands, they found the one they wanted. I stepped across the rows to where the girls were guarding their find. It was half their height and looked like it weighed a ton. "Help!" we yelled together. It took two tall men to get the pumpkin to the car, where it took up half the space in the cavernous trunk of the Continental.

The girls carved a grimace on its enormous face that dared trick or treaters to climb the steps of our Cincinnati Victorian home. When the jack-o'-lantern was installed on the top step of the red-painted front porch, it was the envy of the neighborhood. The home's beveled, leaded glass front door and the colorful stained-glass transoms shined a bit brighter with the glow from the giant pumpkin. The pumpkin's expression resonated with self-importance, like Freddie.

This new man friend gave our fractured family attention. He began taking us to the grocery store, placing fine cuts of meat and tasty vegetables into the cart along with a dozen red roses and a box of Godiva chocolates. His attention was flattering. I felt the possibility of healing from the loss of my first marriage.

31. Johnny's Brooklyn Backyard

FREDDIE CAME OFTEN TO SEE MY DAUGHTERS AND ME at our home in Clifton, close to the University of Cincinnati. He played my spinet piano and sang in a sweet Irish tenor voice. "*Oh, Danny Boy, the pipes, the pipes are playyyyinngggg…*" And he sang, "*When Irish eyes are smiling… when you were sweet… when you were sweet… thirty-three.*" I loved his sweet tenor voice and how he modified the lyrics to catch my attention. In his visits, he began to dribble out the stories of his childhood. The interesting man of the singles and divorced group whom I met as Freddie McMurray was not born with that moniker. His parents, Emilyna, and Henry Soderstrom, named the baby "Johnny," John Walter Soderstrom. For this chapter only, I will refer to Freddie by using his childhood name of Johnny.

Henry divorced Emilyna because he claimed he was sterile from nerve gas used in WWI and insisted she had become pregnant from an affair. Emilyna became a single parent, rearing Johnny the best way she could. Employed as a switchboard operator at the Seagram Company on Park Avenue, Emilyna worked in a large room with many other voices, plugging cords here and there as lights flashed on the board. She hired babysitters to care for Johnny while she was at work. Emilyna and Johnny lived off Flatbush Avenue in Brooklyn on the fourth floor of a brick walk-up. The building superintendent, known as "the Sup," took care of the maintenance, fixed mechanical failures, and accepted their monthly rent check. Johnny's neighbors were Italian, Irish, Jewish, and Chinese, whereas in Riverdale, Dayton, Ohio, where I grew up, we all looked alike. Johnny took Boy Scout camping trips to the woods which terrified him. As he told me more of his childhood days in Brooklyn, I accepted these tales as true.

Superman. Johnny had a buddy in Stanley Katz. Stanley, who had an official Superman cape, wanted to fly just like his hero. Encouraged by Johnny to give his cape a try, Stanley perched on his second-story windowsill, and with his cape flung like wings, he took flight. Gravity did not support his dream, and instead of flying over housetops, he fell to the sidewalk and broke his arm.

The Brooklyn Art Museum. Johnny and his buddies climbed over the fence and headed to the fishpond stocked with golden Japanese coy. The boys stripped and dove in for an evening swim; the water felt cool after closing hours on a summer day. They managed to keep their voices down and were never discovered. After their swim, they pulled themselves out of the pond, dressed, climbed back over the fence, and went home to dinner.

Brooklyn Boys Choir. Johnny had a boy's soprano voice and was a member of the New York City Boys Choir. He was a chunky kid, which added girth and volume to his voice. He was granted voice lessons by an unknown benefactor who recognized his talent in music.

Babysitters. One of his babysitters was an Italian family who ran a gambling business in their 4th-floor walk-up at Tenth and Flatbush. Johnny quietly observed the activities in the apartment. One day after school, Johnny approached the closed door and in his best firm and focused stage voice, knocked boldly at the door. "Open up. This is the police." Inside, he heard the rustle of papers and the flushing of a toilet. Finally, the door was opened to a small schoolboy who stood half the height of the voice of the policeman they thought they had heard from inside. They looked down at the boy. The boy looked up at them. As they looked to the right and to the left, there was no policeman in sight. They had just flushed the days' receipts. Johnny's mother found another sitter.

The Jewish sisters. Johnny was placed in the home of two rotund Jewish sisters who loved to share a daily pastry with the boy. Besides Cream Danish, the sisters bought a heavy, dark, raisin, rye loaf, purchased by the pound, which tasted as if you were sinking your teeth into richness of the Old Country. Best of all, the sisters took him to Radio City Music Hall, where he heard the grand organ before the opening act of the Rockettes. When the Rockettes completed their dazzling routine in a long, high-kicking line across the stage, the house darkened for the movie of the day. Johnny absorbed the sisters' devoted attention and internalized their tasty lifestyle.

Chemistry project. While his mother was at work and he was home on his own after school, he tried his hand at a chemistry project in the kitchen. Using a Bunsen burner, he boiled liquid from his mother's bottle of chlorine bleach. Vapors escaped the test tube which smelled terrible. He turned off the experiment, but not before the chlorine gas escaped, forming a cloud in the kitchen. When it dissipated, he saw that the flowers of the patterned wallpaper were no longer visible. The Sup was not happy with the science experiment. It was time for Johnny and his mother to find the next apartment.

Bronx High School of Science. Johnny took the subway to school, which he attended with students of Chinese and Jewish heritage, along with others who had excelled—the smartest kids of the Boroughs. There was stiff competition and Johnny worked hard, yet always diverting to the unusual, the clever angle of the argument, the how-do-I-outsmart-the-smartest? ...

As Freddie shared his youthful stories of "Johnny" growing up in Brooklyn, it massaged the memories of my own introduction to the city's culture. My introduction to New York City came as a rite-of-passage when I was thirteen years old. My parents put me on a train in the stately art deco train station of Dayton, Ohio, and I traveled solo to the city, where Aunt Lois, my father's sister, and Uncle Irl met me in Penn Station. The three of us boarded the subway, which became an elevated train above the city streets as we rode to their 5th floor World War II rent-protected apartment in the Borough of Queens. I went to sleep that night with the rumble of the elevated, a block away from my bedroom window. Beside the walk-up, there was an old iron elevator that rocked and swayed as it slowly rose to the fifth floor. Riding the elevator was like being on a ride at the amusement park, without the speed.

Aunt Lois gave lessons on her grand piano in their large living room, where oriental carpets graced the wood floor. Appropriate to Aunt Lois's (and my father's) Scottish heritage, afternoon tea was served on a linen tablecloth in delicate porcelain teacups with shortbread cookies and raisin tarts. Aunt Lois, Uncle Irl, and I rode the train into Manhattan to Radio City Music Hall. I remember the magnificent Rockettes, the organ music, and the movie *Fanny*. Aunt and Uncle's Religious Science Church service convened at Carnegie Hall, where I met Dr. Barker, their pastor. We visited Rockefeller Center, walked Fifth Avenue, and rode the elevator to the Empire State Building Observation Tower, where I viewed the city from the top.

I compared Freddie's exciting story renditions of "Johnny" in Brooklyn to my sturdy, day-to-day grounding in the Midwest. I was taken in by the glittery visuals of Times Square. Just like kids who dream of running away with the circus, the energy of the city, the movement of the stories, and the music of his voice were romancing me. I was seduced.

32.Interesting Man

"I CHANGE JOBS ABOUT EVERY FIVE YEARS," Freddie told me. "I get bored and want to move on, try a new job in a different city. Life with me will always be filled with adventure." I thought his tales of adventure sounded intriguing and began to imagine what that might look like. At the time I met Freddie, he was the national energy advisor for a large department store federation, headquartered in Cincinnati with stores across the country from New York, Boston, and Miami to Houston and Los Angeles. I liked to travel, so these possibilities sounded okay. Freddie told me he had a BS, MS, and Ph.D. in Mechanical Engineering from Northwestern University so his quick mind matched his education. Freddie 's business friends liked him, and he sang for their weddings and bar mitzvahs.

His mother was experiencing dementia, and I remember not a single conversation with her that made any sense. Of his other relatives, I met only Aunt Kitty who was close to one-hundred-years old and had retired to Miami. Aunt Kitty had no illuminating stories to supplement Freddie 's renditions. In fact, she had few stories that included him. Knowing very little about Freddie, except his childhood adventure tales, his outward appearance, and his singing, I began to think of the possibilities of marriage.

My attorney friend intervened. "You can't marry Freddie until he is divorced from Marlene, his common law second wife."

"But Freddie told me he was never married to Marlene." I did not want to think I was dating a married man. My friend explained.

"In Kentucky, if you show two names on your checkbook and if you spend nights with each other, publicly declaring your relationship, you have a common-law marriage. If you have a child by that relationship, then you must file for divorce. Before you marry Freddie McMurray, he must file for divorce from Marlene."

I confronted Freddie. "I want the truth. You told me your first wife, Lucinda, was deceased and that you and Marlene never married. You were legally married by common law to Marlene, and she got pregnant and gave birth to your son. Explain."

"I didn't know about common law in Kentucky," he replied. "Since we never went through a ceremony, I didn't think we were ever married. Honest. Believe me. I have only honorable intentions toward you."

Freddie was asking me to be wife number three. I rationalized how he thought he was not legally married and without further questioning, I accepted his explanation. Dutifully, Freddie applied for a divorce from Marlene. Within a year of meeting him at the Methodist Church, Freddie asked me to marry him. Due to Freddie's interests, education, and income, I could look ahead to a secure and satisfying future. I envisioned our days filled with music. I said "yes."

The wedding took place in the same Methodist church. My artist friend, Sandra, silk-screened the invitations. Tracy, a friend of Freddie's at the Lutheran Church where Freddie frequently sang tenor solo, was our organist. My sister-in-law, a musician, was Tracy's assistant. My brother was the usher. Flowers were arranged by my business partner, Karen, gathered from her neighbors' gardens. The councilman, for whom I worked, and the city manager were guests and witnesses, and my lawyer, well known for her gourmet cooking, hosted the reception with an impressive buffet. Mother and my sisters-in-law drove from Dayton for the event.

After my marriage to Freddie, I became the stepmother to his son, Jonathan, who was living with his great grandmother in Kentucky. Together, Freddie and I had three children to rear—my daughters, now ages seven and four, and his son, age five. I looked forward to parenting our expanded family.

For our honeymoon, Freddie and I flew to Los Angeles where we stayed in a home in Beverly Hills, owned by a contractor friend of Freddie's. Built on a hill overlooking the Los Angeles valley, the house had a Hollywood-style swimming pool and house staff. The bedroom could have accommodated all our bedrooms at home. Our bags looked lonely in two large walk-in closets. I felt as though I was being eased into a glamorous life. It seemed distant from the southern Ohio country my grandfather had farmed, distant from the forests in which I had camped as a young girl scout, distant from the rustic, top-of-the-mountain log cabin on the Appalachian Train where Ken and I spent my first honeymoon, far distant from the clay floor home in Brazil where Ken and I had lived. The upscale life Freddie was showing me was interesting. I could become accustomed to extravagant living. I felt like I was floating above the earth, unsettled, but okay. To what was I committed? In November 1977, daughter Emily was born. The older sisters were curious and seemed pleased to have a younger sibling.

33. Alias, Inc.

"HAVE YOU SEEN *The French Connection?*" Freddie asked with a sly smile.

'No, but I've heard of it, I responded." Freddie explains:

"It's a story of a pair of NYC cops in the Narcotics Bureau who stumble onto drug smuggling with a French connection. The main characters are Popeye the detective, Frog One the Frenchman, and Popeye's partner, whom Popeye accidentally shoots and kills, thinking he is Frog One. The movie has a fast-moving car chase through the columns of the elevated train in Queens. Within the movie is a teenage whiz kid from Brooklyn who tests and confirms the purity of heroin in a chemical laboratory before the drug deal can go down. Well, I was that whiz kid. I worked for the Family at the time.

"What do you mean by the Family," I asked, thinking of another movie, *The Godfather.* Freddie continued with his story:

"Working for the Family had its benefits. They needed my brain power. I craved family connection. It was that simple. Testing heroin was alright because I was working with chemistry, and I liked that. But my relationship with the Family came to a point where I needed to make a change. Had to do something different because I was getting older. The police picked me up one day and took me to the station. Gave me a briefing on what would come next. I don't know how the police knew where I was. I guess they kept track of my birth date as well as amassing charges against me. This is what the cop said to me:

"Hey, kid. We know who you are. You have a long history with us, and you have gotten away with a lot of bad behavior. We know you work as a minor for the Family. But come September 24, you will be eighteen, and we'll get you as an adult. We're keeping track, and you'll do time at the Big

House. But… we're going to offer you some options. The Marshall Service can change your identity for an exchange of information on your buddies in the Family. After you squeal, the Marshall Service can sprint you out of town undercover, start you out again with a different name in another town. Now…to repeat…when you turn eighteen, you will be fair game to the police, and you'll be looking at time in prison. Think about it. You have from now 'till your birthday to decide."

"That message got to me. I knew the cops were serious. I thought I was immune to capture. I began to fear that the police were looking at me a bit too closely, and it would be smart to avoid their plan to put me in prison. I needed a way out of the Family. If the police and the Marshall Service could change my identity, why couldn't I do the same?"

I was fascinated, kept quiet, didn't ask any questions to verify or clarify what I was hearing. I just listened. Freddie had more to say:

"My first try at an identity switch was in Brooklyn. I decided to become an Italian since I had Italian kid friends in the neighborhood. I became Joe Benetta. I thought by the time I played out this identity and left Brooklyn, I could leave Joe behind and try another identity. Joe would be a warm-up gig. It worked okay. One time, though, I got caught with the Joe Benetta identity by someone I had known in Brooklyn. I had to act my way out of it. While on a flight with my first wife Lucinda, it caught me by surprise. I'll describe the conversation:"

A former Brooklyn drinking buddy: "Hey, you're Joe Benetta. It's good to see you. How have you been?"

Freddie: "I'm not Joe Benetta. You must be mistaken."

Buddy: "You're joking, of course. You're Joe. Remember how we used to hang out together? We had drinks over at Miki's."

Freddie: "I am not Joe Benetta."

Buddy: "Of course you are. I would know that eye twitch anywhere."

Freddie: "I am not Joe Benetta."

Buddy: "Have it your way, pal." Shaking his head in dismay and sure he had nailed Joe, the man went back to his seat and talked to his partner about the strange encounter.

"When I left Brooklyn, I wanted to fit in, blend, look like everyone else. So, I dropped the Joseph Benetta alias and didn't go back to the name Johnny Soderstrom either. McMurray was a good Celtic name. I liked the sound of it, so switching Johnny and Joe for Freddie sounded good. It suited me. If I could be associated with the personality of a Scotch/Irish gentleman, I would be a good person."

"One of my first jobs trying out the name Freddie McMurray was for an oil company in upstate NY. That's where I met Lucinda—in the company's library. The library was my place of refuge. Growing up in Brooklyn, the library gave me an education. In the company library, Lucinda and I became good friends. She coached me on my vocabulary and grammar as well as diction, and I slowly deleted the street slang of Brooklyn to sound like an educated New Yorker. Brooklynese only returns when I slip back into the Borough and need to be a native speaker. Lucinda taught me how to research Who's Who in America. All the information I needed for a new identity was in the public information section of the library. The library, you remember, was founded by Benjamin Franklin. Open to all. Free. With Lucinda's coaching, I evolved into the smart businessman I am today."

Freddie's stories were getting weird and weirder. If he were wearing a mask façade, then I think, his mask was beginning to crack. It had been two years since our glamorous honeymoon in Beverly Hills. Settling into our roles in marriage, the identity story began to leak from Freddie's controlled behavior. When I married Freddie McMurray, I became Mrs. Freddie McMurray. Not Mrs. Joseph Benetta. Not Mrs. Johnny Soderstrum. Who is wearing a mask—Freddie McMurray or me? I was confused as I tried to make sense of his stories from my own perspective of growing up in a simpler life in Dayton. He had been a bad boy in the streets of Brooklyn but had parlayed the experience into becoming a successful businessman, or had he become successful? Maybe a con. I was afraid of what I did not know…and intrigued.

34. Next Adventure

THESE EARLY YEARS OF MARRIAGE included music, laughter, flowers, fine restaurants, family gourmet meals, and trips to New York City. When we as a family went to New York on business with Freddie, we stayed at the Waldorf-Astoria on Park Avenue and had lunch at the Bull and Bear. The restaurant sported a dark masculine décor, with a stock market ticker tape running across the wall, listing updated trades, giving light to the dark interior. Freddie seemed comfortable in New York City where he knew his way around. These are the memories to NYC, many taken after our move to Richmond, Virginia:

The Waldorf Astoria. We are here for breakfast. When daughter Emily was too little to reach the table, our attentive waiter from Pakistan piled pressed white linen tablecloths into a chair to bring her height up to table level and then pour a glass of milk two feet above the glass without splashing a drop. We were treated as royal guests.

Walking in Manhattan. We laughed when we walked so much that we said we would wear out the soles of our shoes. We walked uptown to a German meat market on the Upper East Side, took the subway south and walked around Fulton Fish Market at the bottom of Manhattan. The catch came to market at the beginning of day, laid out in wooden crates of crushed ice, and selected by the best restaurants for their daily menu.

Emily's curiosity. Emily lost herself when exploring the environment. We visited the Natural History Museum in New York. If I spent too much time studying an exhibit and thinking Emily was beside me, she often slipped away. Retracing my steps, I eventually found her waiting with the guard at the front door. She knew I would look for her there. This practice of exploring the world, following where her curiosity led her, was a constant worry for me. Fortunately, she loved to read, so by positioning her with a book, I knew where she was. However, in the natural history museum, Emily explored where the exhibits led her.

Smith and Wollensky. I remember eating a scrumptious meal here, and every table filled with happy customers.

"This is the best creamed spinach I have ever tasted!" I exclaimed.

"I'm so glad to have joined your family, Barbara. This is such delightful wine and tender steak," said my BFF Ann from Ohio, who had bused into the city to join us for dinner.

"And we can order anything we want," my daughters chimed in.

We talked, ate, and laughed until it was well past the children's bedtime.

Staten Island Ferry. We took the ferry from Battery Park to Staten Island and back. Crossed in front of The Statue of Liberty, stopped, visited, and climbed the steps up to her crown, sharing stories of how some of our ancestors might have come to this country by way of this passage.

Taps on mosaic tiles. I remember Emily, age four, was fascinated by the pattern of mosaic floor tiles at the entrance to the Waldorf Astoria. She broke into a spontaneous tap dance as if trained for this moment. The sound of her rhythmic taps filled the upper lobby. People stopped and backed away to give Emily space to dance in her maroon velvet long pants and white shirt. They must have thought they were witnessing a child star. Satisfying herself that she had experimented with the auditory connection of heels to tile, Emily turned to the wide, highly polished handrail of the staircase leading down to the exit on Park Avenue. She mounted the rail as if it were her horse and slid down the entire two flights. A mature, elegantly dressed lady stuck her nose in the air at such behavior. Freddie noticed the lady's disagreeable posture, went to the handrail, swung his leg over it, and followed Emily to the bottom of the staircase. It was all I could do not to follow and enjoy the slide myself. Wearing a skirt, I thought I would not be able to slide so easily.

Operatic arias. In our own home, I remember hearing Freddie 's Irish tenor voice singing arias from La Boehme, Rigoletto, and Turandot. When he put on a 33-rpm record of Pavarotti, the living room became a concert hall. With his arms raised, he directed the music, accompanied by his own voice—strong, yet tender, singing of love. I absorbed the love solos, assuming they were meant for me.

When Freddie was ready to leave the company in Cincinnati, he looked for retail jobs in Texas and Virginia. Deciding between them, he asked me to fly to Richmond and look for a house. I did not know why he was leaving his current job, nor did he give me a reason other than he was ready for the next adventure.

Three years into my second marriage and on Emily's first birthday, the family packed the car, crossed the Ohio River into Kentucky, and flew from the Greater Cincinnati Airport to Richmond, Virginia, on the James River, the Confederate Capital. Statues of Confederate generals adorned Monument Avenue with its antebellum mansions and its handmade, hand-laid, red-brick street. The move from Cincinnati to Richmond was not only a cultural change from North to South, but it also took Suellen and Audrey states away from their father, making visitation for Ken a much less frequent happening. I did not ask the tough questions; I followed my husband to his new job.

35. A Chameleon Adapts to New Environment

Richmond 1978

A RETAIL COMPANY, started by a peddler with a sack on his back at the time of the Civil War, was seeking an Energy Management Director to build new stores in Charleston, South Carolina, Virginia Beach and Midlothian, Virginia. Freddie's resume fit the job description, and he was offered the job headquartered in Richmond. In this position, he hosted a national energy managers' meeting and bused the attending engineers to Virginia Beach to see his new HVAC (Heating, Ventilation, Air Conditioning) system perched on the roof of a new store. He offered drinks and snacks in route, and the engineers had a good time. I remember another weekend when the family joined Freddie for a trip to New York City. I offered to take Mary, Emily's daycare teacher, with us.

Given only a two-hour notice, Mary grabbed a bag and hopped into the car. Originally from Alabama, Mary had never been north of Richmond, so the trip was an adventure into the country north of the Mason Dixon line. As was our custom, the family stayed at the Waldorf Astoria. Mary took the girls for a walk to Central Park, stopping along the way to purchase hot dogs at the Sabrett vendor stand on 5th Avenue. She returned to the hotel with tales of the outing. "New Yorkers are friendly. When I asked for directions, they offered to help. And I was not mugged." The Deep South met Yankee North with good outcomes. It was all in communication, listening and respecting each other.

Learning the language and pace of Richmond was different from New York City. Freddie McMurray, the New Yorker businessman, would speak rapidly with a prepared agenda to cover all important details, much like the pace of walking the New York City blocks to cover distance on the grid. Transplanting a New Yorker to Richmond, Virginia via Cincinnati, Ohio was an adjustment. He needed to take a deep breath, slow down, relax, inquire about family and current events, be interested and sociable, and discuss whatever is not business... until near the end of the conversation. Then, and only then, is important business brought up, and settled.

Freddie 's first wife, Lucinda, had assisted Freddie in elevating his Brooklyn Street language into New York business speech. But in Richmond, the Old South, home of the Confederacy, Freddie learned a different language—to show respect for southern military, draw out the conversation, and always, as it was a ritual ahead of any business, enquiring about the family.

If you were to apply this same standard of conversation ritual and ask what was happening within the family of the Freddie McMurray household in Bon Air, and if you engaged in an honest conversation and truly listened, the revelations would be horrifying. If we could be the guardian eye that looked through the roof and between the walls, we would see behaviors that would take our breath away.

In the well-appointed dining room of our southern home, landscaped among blooming pink and white dogwood trees, flowering purple, pink, and fuchsia-colored rhododendron bushes, and shiny green leaf holly, daughters Suellen and Audrey approach me. They ask me to listen. Now ages nine and twelve, they have collaborated in a plan to inform me of their stepfather's abuse. It is time to tell. It should have happened sooner, but this afternoon, they put their plan in front of me.

"Freddie raped me," says nine-year-old Audrey. Suellen sits close by, watching my reaction,

"Surely you don't mean that. I can't imagine you even know the meaning of the word. Freddie loves you. Maybe he has a hard time expressing it." Shocked at this revelation, I spoke much too quickly when I should have been silent and listened. I could not imagine abuse happening within my home. Maybe someone else's home but not mine, not here, not now. My mind could not comprehend what the girls were saying. My brain would not accept the information. With my family of origin, I had never heard of sexual abuse, and I could not believe it existed here. I failed to ask questions, afraid to hear more. Instead, I shut down in shock and disbelief. Audrey and Suellen did not elaborate.

Their plan to inform me I cut short, tabled, yet stored in the recesses of my brain. Sexual abuse within my family? It just wasn't possible. It couldn't be true. I walk to the kitchen to prepare dinner, something I know how to do well, something I could do without thinking. Life goes on as if the revelation of sexual abuse to my daughters never took place.

36. Chameleon Moves Again

1982

IN LESS THAN FIVE YEARS, the Richmond retail company released Freddie. When Freddie departed the company, he set up his own consulting services and called his new company Corporate Energy Management. The CEO of his former retail company provided him with a letter that said. "We recommend Dr. McMurray, and we will be first in line for his services." Freddie never heard from the retail company again. I became Corporate Energy Management's secretary and writer of promotional literature. It was about this time that I drove to King County Hospital in Brooklyn to retrieve Freddie's mother and move her to Richmond to live with us. She had Alzheimer's Dementia.

One of the companies for whom Freddie consulted in his new business was a national convenience chain store, headquartered in Houston. The company was impressed with the consultation and asked Freddie to be their National Energy Director. We packed our household items to move to Houston, along with two cats and Grandma Emilyna, who. continued her slow decline with dementia.

We said goodbye to friends: Emily's daycare teacher, Mary, her pre-school friend Jason and Jason's mom, Emily's favorite climbing trees. Suellen said goodbye to a boyfriend after a swim in the James River, and daughter Audrey to her Girl Scout buddies. I said goodbye to the azaleas I had planted, the rhododendrons, and dogwood. I would miss the lovely row of holly down the driveway and the gentleness of life in Virginia. We tucked away memories, left our Southern friends, and headed to the state of Texas, not knowing what the next adventure would bring.

37. Chameleon Slithers to Cypress Creek

Houston 1982

THE COMPANY CONVENIENCE STORES were branded by red, green, and yellow traffic light signs at each store location, nationwide. Suellen was starting high school; Audrey, middle school; and Emily, first grade. We found a five-bedroom home on Little Cypress Creek that fit us all, Grandma Emilyna and cats included. Next to a pipeline company park, it was a spacious rural development with no sidewalks. Tall Eastern Pines wooded the deep backyard leaving long pine needles strewn across the grass, needles that could be woven into baskets. Behind the garage was a large woodpile of old and rotting timber. We stayed the first night in a nearby motel due to a power outage, a few days after Hurricane Alicia.

Adventures started early in Texas. Before visiting our new home, Grandma unlocked her motel room door and walked off into the night. She found her way across the overpass of the 12-lane Northwest Freeway. Police found her wandering and took her to a nearby long-term care facility, where we retrieved her.

The next day, we arrived to inspect our new home, piling out of the car to survey our new home recently impacted by Hurricane Alicia. We found the back gate pushed in two feet and leaning. A four-foot black water moccasin slithered down the back step into the bushes. A neighbor crossed the street to question our presence. He had two tall grey Weimaraner guard dogs and he cradled a shotgun.

"Can I help you?" he inquired.

"We're visiting our new home." Freddie responded, "Are you the welcome committee?"

After moving into the house, Emily visited a neighbor to introduce herself and was attacked by their dog, slashing her lower lip. Not knowing the medical community, I resorted to the nearest clinic in Tomball where an on-call doctor from East India sutured her lip under protest, without anesthesia. Emily bears the scar today.

38. Purple Ruffles #MeToo

1985

"EVERYONE KNOWS BUT YOU."

I had my head bowed over my mother's seventy-year-old feather-weight Singer Sewing Machine, pushing five yards of purple netting under the pressure foot, gathering the fabric into an elastic waistband. The gown would be for my daughter's high school formal band dance. Old Singer was humming along at an experienced worker's pace as I focused on holding the fabric to the half-inch marker. Speaking with increased intensity and purpose, Suellen directed her words to me in my prayerful position.

"Everyone knows but you," she repeated.

I paused. The presser foot stopped in the up position. Suellen was silent, waiting.

What didn't I know? The mortgage was up to date. The horse was not sick with colic. Freddie was still employed; my part-time school nurse job was intact. I didn't like playing this guessing game. Could not my daughter provide a few details instead of innuendo? Yet, I felt in her words an intense pain, something primal activating my maternal instincts. It took my breath away. I felt fear in my gut, that I had to face what I had hoped for so long was not true.

My mind flashed to a visit in the Florida Everglades last year when the nature guide told us after baby alligators were hatched, mother alligators kept watch for an entire year to protect them from the father who would eat the young as fresh, moving food. I thought of the sacred relationship husband and wife and the protective care of the young they share. I keenly felt my daughter's words ripping my soul.

"Everyone knows but you," she said for the third time.

"Do you mean…?"

"Yes, he got my sister, too—when she was little, shortly after you married Freddie. We tried to tell you four years ago when we lived in Richmond. You didn't believe us then, so we didn't talk about it after that. Kept it to ourselves, until now. Audrey and I want you to believe us."

"Yes, I remember that you tried to talk to me. I couldn't understand and did not want to believe it, so I shut down and put it away, so I didn't have to think about it. It was too awful. Now, I hear you and feel our pain and my own pain for not accepting what you were trying to tell me. I didn't ask questions. I avoided the subject and tucked the conversation away as if it did not happen."

"Freddie has not abused Audrey and me since we moved to Texas three years ago, but Emily is now the age of Audrey when he first abused her. We want you to protect Emily.

"What should I do?" I asked.

"I don't know," Suellen answered.

"What can I do?"

"I don't know," she answered again.

I sat in silence, for what seemed an eternity. I heard the back door open downstairs, Freddie returning home from work. Only then did I leave Suellen's room.

"Freddie, you have abused the girls."

"Barbara, I would not do that. I love the girls, all three." Freddie was adamant in his denial. He reversed the accusation as if I were imaging the

140

disclosure, minimizing the topic for discussion, accusing me of fantasizing. His manner of speaking and words were strong, convincing, rehearsed. Messages in my mind jumbled, and I began to prepare our dinner as if I were working remotely. In the days that followed, I felt as though I was kicked in the stomach and couldn't breathe. Suellen's words reverberated in my brain. I asked the family to go to family counseling.

"No," said the girls.

"Yes," said Freddie.

Where do I turn for help? I had a good relationship with Emily's grade school counselor, Mrs. Green. She had helped Emily to adjust to the concept of an open classroom when what Emily needed was structure. She had counseled when Emily acted out inappropriately. She had called a team conference when Emily struck the principal, her authority figure. Picking up the phone, I dialed Counselor Green. "I can recommend Mr. Todd, the assistant minister of the local Methodist Church," she said.

We had been attending the services at the Methodist Church. I was unaware of this assistant minister, but I accepted Mrs. Green's recommendation and called for a family counseling appointment.

The church conference room had one chair on the end of a rectangular table where the counselor sat. Freddie and I sat facing each other on opposite sides of the table, making a triangle. For a church classroom, this room was notably devoid of pictures of Jesus helping little children. No Bible psalms on the wall. No vases filled with artificial flowers or palm fronds.

Mr. Todd looked like an official clergyman in a dark suit jacket, white shirt open at the neck as if trying to be casual. He was youthful and his clean-shaven face was clear of blemishes. He had heavy black eyebrows against a pale face. I would lose him in a line-up. Mr. Todd explained how he would conduct the counseling session. He would open the session with us both together to understand the issue between us. Then he would see each of us separately, in what he called an individual caucus. After caucus time, the three of us would reconvene for a closure. Freddie and I agreed to this format.

I spoke first. "My daughters have revealed Freddie sexually abused them, and Emily, the youngest sister, is at the age now when the abuse began, soon after I married Freddie. I did not know this had happened until recently."

Mr. Todd turned to Freddie. "How do you respond?"

"I did not abuse them. The girls miss their father. I try to be a good stepfather, and I certainly do not want them to forget their father. We have moved further away, which makes it difficult for their father to see them."

Time for caucus. Freddie left the room leaving me alone with Mr. Todd. I began explaining that my oldest daughter, now age fifteen, revealed Freddie's sexual abuse began when she was seven and for her sister, age five. The abuse with the two older girls continued after the move to Richmond but has not continued since the move to Texas. I do not know if Freddie has abused our daughter Emily, but she's had disciplinary problems at school, including assaulting the principal. Emily is taking Ritalin for ADD, Attention Deficit Disorder, which the school nurse supervises, is picked up by the special needs bus and transported to another school for a class in behavior modification.

The minister counselor was quiet through my disclosure, saying little and not asking questions. Freddie and I switched places, and I took a seat in the hallway several classroom doors from the conference room. I sat on a vinyl-covered loveseat facing the wall with pictures one would expect to see in the Methodist Church. One was a picture of the head of Jesus with long brownish-red hair, his kind eyes looking up as if in wonder of the heavens. Another was a scene of John the Baptist and Jesus gathering at the river for baptism. A third was of Jesus dressed in a long flowing white robe, sitting on a rock, surrounded by small children who looked up to him. A small stand, supporting a large vase of artificial red geraniums, was set under the Jesus and children painting.

When Freddie 's private session was over, I was called back in for the closing conference. I had no idea what Freddie had discussed with Mr. Todd, but I was surprised to feel that I was the one excluded, on the outs, as if I had been the accused party and what I had disclosed had no validity. Mr. Todd began. "Freddie thinks you are a saint, speaks well of your work at home and with the school district. He told me about your move to Texas and how you set up home here."

The closing session was that—closure. Nothing was mentioned from our separate sessions. The minister might have interviewed the girls separately, but he made no mention of doing so. Nor did Mr. Todd suggest another session for Freddie and me. He left me hanging as if my revelation was a fantasy and the abuse did not happen. Session ended.

I was again floating above the earth looking for a grounding. As I left the pale-faced minister in the bland conference room, it felt colder than when I entered. My daughters had put their trust in me to speak. Was domestic violence not a subject one could discuss? Could there be a conspiracy of secrecy? Why is it when I finally broached the subject and had the courage to put it on the table, I was the intruder into the club? I did not know what to do next or whom to believe or whom to trust with my disclosure. If the Methodist minister did not believe me, whom could I trust? Family members returned to work, school, activities, and the issue of sexual abuse was shelved, but it remained a festering blister in my brain.

39. Released

1986

FREDDIE HAD BEEN WITH THE CONVENIENCE STORE CHAIN five years. He asked me to go to his office to pick up his personal belongings – family pictures and such, telling me nothing about why he was leaving his job. Why didn't Freddie go himself? Why ask me to go in this place? Always ready to help someone in need, and not asking questions, I agreed to go. I asked my neighbor, Larry, husband to my early morning walking partner, to go with me. I wanted company and needed help with boxes.

Early Sunday morning, after a forty-five-minute drive into Houston, Larry and I met the CEO and the chief security officer at the front door of the convenience store headquarters. The two men led us to Freddie's office. As I began to fill boxes with family photos and personal papers, the CEO and security officer stood by, watching carefully. Larry was nearby, supportive. I felt as if I were guilty of something; yet, knew it was not about me, but I felt defensive, intimidated by what I did not know, and afraid to ask. Those in the room were silent as I worked. The space felt spooky, creepy, dishonest. Is this the way company execs dispose of personnel? I wanted to ask. When I had gathered Freddie 's belongings, Larry and I were escorted to the front door. The building was locked behind us.

Larry and I made small talk on the way home, filling the awkward space between us. I felt I was driving down a Texas freeway on a tram in the fog, not knowing if we would stay on track. When I reached home safely and I was alone with Freddie, I asked, "What was that all about?" Silence was the response.

Many years later, long after I divorced, left Freddie McMurray in Texas, and moved across the country, I was referred to an article in a detective trade journal that spoke of a Freddie McMurray creating a business plan that would install fake energy-saving units on the roof of every convenience store in the company. It would have bilked the company of billions, the article said. As I read the article, I thought I recognized the name attributed to the vendor of energy units, thinking it might have been a person I met in California at the time of our honeymoon. I could not be sure. Was the Freddie McMurray mentioned in the article the same as my husband Freddie McMurray?

40. Crafted Resume

THE HOUSTON PUBLIC LIBRARY was promoting an Aztec mask exhibit I wanted to see. Freddie asked to go with me, "to do research," he said. "I'll show you how to study "*Who's Who in American Engineering.*"

Freddie located thickly bound volumes of *Who's Who* and carried them to a long wooden table to begin his research. Thinking back to my college days, I recalled receiving the promotional brochure for *Who's Who in Nursing* when I was a graduate, inviting me to join. I remember this listing would be valuable to me as I climbed the ladder in my professional career and would cost one hundred dollars. As a new graduate, I couldn't afford the entrance fee, so I didn't complete the application. My attention returned to what Freddie was explaining. "There are hundreds of listings of *Who's Who* in various fields of engineering with the name of Freddie McMurray," he said. "All the listings have their educational and work history.

Shaking my head like the man on the plane who recognized Freddie as Joe Benetta, I turned away and returned to the study of the Aztec masks, pondering. Does he wear a mask? Could I be wearing a mask?

Ten years earlier than this library visit, and soon after I married Freddie McMurray in Cincinnati, his second ex (common law) wife Marlene came to visit. At that time, Freddie and I were happily blending our family—his son Jon and my daughters, Audrey and Suellen. Marlene stood on the porch just outside the back door and talked to me in the kitchen while I was preparing dinner for the children. I recall her story. "When Freddie traveled for business, he set up a woman in every city. Because of his philandering, I wanted to search for the possibilities of a new life away from him. I knew our son Jon was not safe in Freddie's care, so I left Jon in the care of my great grandmother who doted on Jon. I left Freddie and went to California to look for work. It provided distance and a pleasant environment. Freddie provided me with a new Ford Taurus to get around."

I was half-listening, focused on the children's dinner. But I began to listen more closely as Marlene's story provided information on Freddie's identity. Marlene was trying to tell me that her life with Freddie McMurray was anything but normal. She was trying to clue me into his background and that she, Marlene, had been living with a fraud—Freddie. I believe now that her intent that evening was a woman-to-woman disclosure, letting me know in my naivete what was beneath the man's facade. What she was telling me was exceedingly difficult to believe. Marlene continued.

"I travelled to his home in Tennessee to alert the real Dr. McMurray that his identity had been stolen. The legitimate Dr. Fred McMurray was a professor and used a middle initial of 'L.' Freddie dropped the middle initial thinking the name was cleaner without it. Fred L. McMurray studied Mechanical Engineering and had a BS, MS, and PhD from Northwestern University."

According to Marlene, nothing came of her encounter with the real Dr. Fred McMurray, who was not inclined to take her seriously. I, too, had a hard time believing what she was telling me. I was a nurse and cared for people. Took them as they were and liked them, including both Freddie and Marlene. How did Freddie have time for a woman in each city he visits? Craziness. No wonder Freddie loved me. I was his commonsense, at-home wife.

Marlene had returned to Cincinnati from California and was planning court action to regain custody of Jonathan. As a blended family, we thought we were exactly right, adjusting well, and did not like the possibility of losing Jonathan. Upon returning from the court hearing, Freddie told me he had to relinquish custody. Marlene had threatened to expose his identity. If he relinquished Jon to her, she would not expose what she knew of his identity theft. That night, Freddie went to sleep with his arms wrapped around Jonathan, trying to forever hold onto his love for this little boy.

The next day, Freddie gathered Jon's clothes and toys. When Marlene's car pulled up, Freddie packed Jonathan's belongings into the car and sadly waved goodbye. We did not see Jonathan again. Freddie's stolen identity remained intact.

Recalling Marlene's visit in another city, I studied the color and design of Aztec masks in the public library of Houston. Why were the masks created? What were they revealing? What was the story they were hiding?

41. Fired, Chameleon Seeks What's Next

FREDDIE HEADED ALONE TO NEW YORK CITY, a place he knew, spoke the language, and rented a fifth-floor, small apartment, barely room enough for one person. A long-term health care facility hired him to inspect the properties. His job lasted seven months. Freddie returned to Texas.

My mother had given me money to buy and train a dog for the family. She suggested a collie, as she had had as a young girl, a dog that loved and roamed the farm with her, an animal she dearly loved. I looked for a collie, but Freddie insisted on a German Shepherd. Mom thought that was okay, and Ootah, a malamute/German Shepherd mix, became our new family member. One evening I saw Freddie on the patio abusing Ootah. Freddie's back was to me, and I saw the opportunity to give him a quick kick in the tush. I took aim. Bullseye. Freddie let go of Ootah but swung around with his arm. His full hand slapped my face, knocking me off balance. Audrey witnessed the scene and began sobbing and ran upstairs to her room. Shocked and wanting to comfort her to comfort me, I climbed the stairs after her. We hugged and sobbed, each in our own pain.

42. New York Bank Account

FREDDIE HAD BUSINESSES ON THE SIDE. I was not sure what they were. Asbestos removal I thought was one. Another was stockpiling old convenience store equipment, finding creative ways to reuse surplus. These businesses, I imagined, were good for the universe. Removing and disposing of toxic materials was admirable in cleaning up the environment and reducing toxic waste. I am an advocate for recycling, finding alternative uses for everything. I deplore throwing something away that has another use. Believing I was contributing to the clean-up of the universe, I became a part-time assistant to Freddie's alternative businesses.

My contribution to the business was an occasional all-in-one-day turnaround trip, Houston to New York City. I left the house at 4:00 AM to catch the first direct flight, landing at J.F.K. International Airport. I boarded the shuttle to Grand Central Station, stepped off the bus at Park and 42nd and walked to the bank. There was a line for each teller, so I stepped into the queue and waited my turn.

Face to face with the teller, I handed her the envelope, which contained a deposit slip and a check for $40,000. I didn't bother to look at the name on the check. Freddie's name was the principal on the bank account. My name and brother's were also on the account. The teller asked no questions, received the check, and stamped it in. Business done.

Next, I was to pick up mail at Freddie's office service. I entered through heavy, steel-framed and glass doors into a spacious, tiled floor lobby with a row of elevators to the left. Exiting on the eighth floor, a bank of receptionists sat behind desks with multiple mail slots behind their backs. I asked for Freddie 's mail. She pulled an envelope with his name, and I placed it in my bag and left.

On the returning flight, I hoped to nap. Instead, my mind wandered to TV mysteries, thinking about how I could sabotage my business trip with matters of self-interest. I could open my own bank account and put the money there, out of the reach of others. I could open the mail and sabotage correspondence. I found it hard to think of such sinister behavior and gave up the idea of trying to write such a script. A nap seemed a better use of flight time. I arrived home well after dinner. The girls were doing homework and preparing for the next school day. I related tales from my quick trip and heard their adventures of the day. It felt good to be home.

43. Chameleon Slithers to Enron

GRANDMA EMILYNA'S DEMENTIA had progressed to the point that she needed 24-hour care. Freddie placed his mother in a nursing home in the Montrose area, downtown Houston. Without the need to be her constant 24/7 caregiver, I was able to pursue work outside the home and return to professional development. When I was hired as a part-time school nurse, I had forgotten how much I missed the stimulation of contributing to the community. It supported independence thinking.

Enron hired Freddie to be an energy management consultant. At first, he told me Exxon hired him. I'm sure that is what he said. It was Enron who hired him, not Exxon. I liked his Enron job because I could travel with Freddie in the protected HOV lane ahead of the rush hour crunch, park for an hour at the Enron garage, workout in their employee's exercise room in the basement of the building, then leave for my job at the health department. At the end of my workday, I returned to Enron to pick Freddie up and head out the Northwest Freeway to home. We developed a rhythm in our commute. The girls, meanwhile, took the school bus or drove, and were developing their own routines, competence, and independence.

Within Enron, Freddie 's office was located among the top executive offices high up in the tower of the company. One morning, Freddie was studying the pipelines crisscrossing the country. A darkened room with lit computer screens at multiple stations tracked the flow of gas across the country. Finishing his study and returning to his own office, he passed an open door of the CEO in which sat a private detective. It happened to be the same detective who tracked Freddie at the convenience store company. I imagine the conversation in the executive's suite went something like this:

Startled detective: "Hey, who is that man?"

CEO: "Why, that's Freddie McMurray, our Energy Management Director."

Detective: "Let me tell you a little history of that employee. I tracked him for a year at his previous place of employment. Turned out he had business on the side of recycling the company's unused store equipment."

After work, I picked up Freddie in front of the Enron building, slumped over his briefcase.

"I've been released."

The drive home up the Northwest Freeway took over an hour. I drove and listened, but Freddie had little to say, only that he now had no job, …again. We had been married thirteen years. Changing colors and adapting to each new environment, like the Chameleon, was getting old. I was tired of his "adventures," adjusting to new social circles, and moving the children to a new school in a new city. This was not the classy life I had envisioned, but one where I had to slink away from friends. I was through with Freddie's adventures.

I believed in the concept of marriage in which you work as a team, a partnership and for the good of the family. Freddie was into self-preservation. His frequent job moves did not support stability. Fortunately, two daughters had their Cincinnati father in their lives, investing his overtimes into visits and who also served as an alternative role model for the youngest daughter.

I was gaining confidence and experience in my professional work. The job with the county health department was challenging as I functioned with an outstanding team of medical and public health professionals. I supervised a communicable disease program and served on a task force to access health care for those who crossed the border into Texas with active cases of tuberculosis. The County and the City of Houston experienced a measles outbreak, second only in severity to Los Angeles County, and I organized immunization clinics in response to the epidemic. Challenged by my work and enjoying professional peers, I was beginning to think that the family would be better off without Freddie and his instability of frequent job moves.

44. My Investments?

"GONE? GONE? The inheritance from my mother's estate, which you so bragged about your brilliance in investing, is gone?" I stared at him in shocked disbelief. Freddie lied about how well our stocks were doing.

On my thirteenth birthday, I had received a share of General Motors stock. The certificate was an impressive piece of paper that would translate into real money over time. That was about it for my understanding of the stock market. I did not ask questions, and we did not discuss finance or investments or even budgeting within the family. I knew little of money matters except saving pennies in the piggy bank when I was a kid.

When my mother died at age 82, she left an inheritance for my sister, brother, and me from her job as a case worker for the county's disabled children. My inheritance was for my children's education. I wanted it invested wisely. Freddie paid attention to the stock market. He bragged about his keen instinct and ability to invest in the right stocks at the right time to increase the value of the portfolio. Freddie asked if I would like him to invest my mother's inheritance. I trusted his ability to make wise choices in line with my family's values. Our stockbroker in Houston was Sam Cashman, a good enough name for a man dealing in money markets.

I was successful at work with the health department. But I felt tension within the family and wanted help in sorting things out. I called Nancy, my friend from college days. We arranged to meet.

"Nancy, we have tension at home. Suellen leaves to spend overnights with friend Rachael. Audrey keeps to herself. Emily goes to the corral to be with her horse. Freddie is antsy and grumpy when he comes home from work. I feel as if I am treading water, trying to tie the family together when there is no string. At the table, we eat in silence as if we were monks. We play our scripts as if on a stage. Suellen is getting ready for college, and I will want to look at selling stocks for tuition."

"Barb, check in with your stockbroker and find out how you did in the recession of '87. Be sure you know how your investments are doing and what is available to you."

"Good idea. I have left the finances to Freddie. I'll call the broker on my own." I called Sam Cashman and asked him the status of my account.

There was silence on the other end of the line.

"Freddie didn't tell you?" Sam asked.

"Freddie didn't tell me what?"

"Barbara, Freddie put your mother's inheritance on a potentially lucrative, but risky stock. The recession intervened. It's gone. Nothing left."

I ended the call, in shock and anger. At home that night, before we could get to dinner, I confronted Freddie.

"Sam Cashman told me today you lost my mother's inheritance on a risky investment, and the stock evaporated with the recession. Worse, you did not tell me the outcome. I trusted you. I believed in your so-called 'ability to invest well.' You were dishonest."

"I didn't tell you because I knew you would be disappointed."

"Disappointed! Disappointed? You lied to me!"

"I am not responsible for what happened. The market caused the loss. Give me credit for trying."

My heart was pounding. Freddie was not embarrassed, sorry, or apologetic. He pooh-poohed my outrage. He didn't care, not even enough to discuss the loss.

45. Briefcase

1989

TEN DAYS BEFORE THIS VERY NIGHT, while Emily and I were delivering Christmas pound cakes to the neighbors on the back of her horse, riding double, her horse threw off the extra weight, and I landed on the ground. Hurting, I needed to go to the Emergency Room. Freddie refused to take me. I drove the ten miles. It hurt to be behind the wheel. Upon examination, I had four fractured ribs. It is now the first weekend of January.

It is 3:00 AM, and I awakened from a deep sleep, not knowing what nudged me to do so. I slip out from under the sheets without making a ruffle and remember Freddie is leaving on a morning flight to New York City. I walk into the family room and head directly to his brown leather briefcase on the coffee table, ready for a quick pick-up in the morning. I had never touched his briefcase. Not ever. But this moment the briefcase beckons to me. Something or someone is guiding me. I open the latches. In the front pocket I see two first class airline tickets to New York City. As if inviting me to have a closer look, they fell into my hands for inspection. Each ticket costs $832. My name is on one of the tickets. My husband's name is on the other. He has not asked me to join him. Replacing the tickets as if they had not been found, I retrace my steps to the bedroom, walking with a determined step while my blood is boiling and my heart beating double time.

In a terse whisper channeled directly into his left ear, I say "I understand that I am going to travel with you today." There was a pause as if his outer ear received the information, funneled it into the inner ear, now traveling across the synapses to the left hemisphere of the frontal cortex, analyzing and interpreting the tone of the inquiry, and calculating a reply. Freddie's eyes opened wide. He threw back the covers, bolted out of bed on the opposite side from me, and fell into the wall trying to regain balance. With the startled awakening, he collected his composure, and I could see him concocting a magnificent lie.

"Well, I knew that you would not be able to travel with your ribs hurting, and Joe's wife was ready for a retreat to the Big Apple. I volunteered to give her an introduction. Call it 'community service' and helping your friends."

"The ticket reads 'Barbara McMurray. Who is Joe? Who is his wife? Why is another woman using my name? Is her name my name?"

I did not expect answers, but I enjoyed asking questions and observing him fumble for something to say. He was grasping for a reasonable response, and I was entertained by his struggle, aware I was in control of the conversation. The lead was in my court, and I took pleasure in the drama.

Freddie avoided eye contact and further conversation. He turned his attention to dressing in his best suit and overpacking a large suitcase with more clothes than he needed for a weekend trip to New York City. He worked quickly, silently, as if trying to leave before he had to say anything more. He wanted his alibi to stick with no need for further embellishment. He exited the back door, revved up the car to handle the chill night air, and left for the airport. It was 4:00 AM. It would be hours before his flight. In his rush, he forgot his long black cashmere coat, something he would need for a freezing weekend in New York City.

I was ticked off, angry, hurt, jealous, shocked, and my ribs hurt. I caught my husband in a lie. and yet I wanted to believe he had some decency left. He bought a first-class ticket for someone using my name, to a city where I would have enjoyed the theater. If this were a pleasure trip, the benefits and luxuries were not coming to me. I thought of the quick one-day trips I had endured in and out of the city. Why would I ever trust him again? I had seen the airline tickets, and in my brain was the nagging acknowledge of abuse. Wasn't this abuse? Why was it so hard for me to accept this reality?

I did not feel like going back to bed. Eyeing the forgotten coat, I bundled myself against the cold, grabbed the coat, and left the house for the airport. Approaching the airline check-in counter where Freddie was the lone passenger, I tapped him on the shoulder. *"You forgot your coat."*

Hearing my voice, he turned. Color left his face, and he stared at me as I stood holding the coat, smiling. I briefly considered hanging out to see the person with the same name as mine. But, feeling I had had enough drama for the middle of the night, I turned to go. Our daughters would be getting up for school, needing breakfast, and Emily needed to be ready for pick-up by the special education school bus. I had parent duties and did not need more confrontation. I returned to my car and headed home... and remembered Neiman-Marcus had advertised a dress sale.

At the end of the weekend, Freddie returned to a quiet home. "I expected to see my clothes thrown out the back door," he said. With the evidence of betrayal, and with the hurt I felt for his cover up, I had not thought of throwing him out of the house. Why didn't I react with more gumption and confront him? Why was I so namby-pamby?

46. Overnight Bag, Packed and Ready

A WEEK LATER, AT 3:00 A.M., I was again fully awake in the night darkness. Sliding out from under the sheet, I moved quietly. This time, the force directed me to my closet, and I packed what I would need for overnight. The new tweed two-piece suit I had purchased the weekend before at the dress sale would be perfect for the office and whatever travel I planned after work. I smiled at the preparation and returned to bed for sleep before the alarm sounded.

Freddie noticed the overnight bag I placed into the trunk of the car.

"What is your bag for?"

"I don't know yet, but I'm prepared. I'll let you know when I know." On a dark and rainy Friday, a beginning to Martin Luther King holiday weekend, we left the house for morning commute into Houston.

At my desk in the health department, work was slow. The boss was gone; meetings, cancelled. I dialed Lois, the travel agent.

"I want to fly to London tonight for under $500 and return Tuesday after the holiday. My sister and her husband are in London on sabbatical. Lockerbie just happened, and someone is going to cancel their ticket. There will be a seat for me."

Half an hour later, Lois returned my call. "I found a ticket on the grey market for $450 plus train ride into Victoria Station. Good luck. Safe travel."

Freddie called and invited me to have lunch at Brennan's. It would give me the opportunity to discuss my weekend plans. When I arrived at Brennan's, Freddie was seated with friend Sam.

"I am flying to London tonight to visit my sister and brother-in-law," I informed them. Freddie was silent, surprised, and began begging me not to go. Sam intervened:

"Oh, my wife does that all the time. She even went to London recently."

Freddie gave up on the begging me not to go and said quietly almost in a whisper. "I guess I had last weekend. You're entitled to this one." Opening his briefcase, he withdrew a freshly minted, wrapped package of five hundred one-dollar bills. Handing me the money, he said, "Enjoy your trip."

"Yes, this is my weekend. I am confident that the girls will be okay, and you are not to mess with them." That afternoon, when I was ready to leave the office, I called home for a chat with Audrey. I told her my four-day itinerary, the plan to visit my sister, and asked her to take care of Emily. Without hesitation and with support for my mission, Audrey answered: "You go, Mom! Yes, I'll take care of Emily."

Before rush hour traffic was in full swing, I headed to the airport, picked up the ticket, parked the car, grabbed the overnight bag, and waited in the flight club. Sitting near me was a gentleman, and upon hearing of my first trip to London, began to inform me where to stay and what to do—the hotel next to Victoria Station, ride the double decker bus, and shop Harrods.

When the airplane lifted from the tarmac, I heard the wheels pull the body of the plane. "I really am on my way to London," I said aloud. I felt free, exhilarated, terrified. Lights of Houston shone like diamonds sparkling against the black night. The gems grew dimmer, the night, darker. A few hours later, the captain announced that we were flying over New York City. I looked out the window to see tiny white specks far below.

Soon, however, we were in total darkness over the Atlantic Ocean, on a trajectory to London. I drifted into sleep. Upon arrival at Gatwick Airport and with only a small overnight bag, customs waved me through. I descended the stairs to the train station and boarded for London.

"Victoria Station, next stop," the conductor announced.

After disembarking, I headed to the iconic red call box and dialed the number of the flat where I thought my sister was living. The front desk receptionist answered the call:

"Your sister was here but checked out. Let me look at the board and see if she left a forwarding number. Yes, here it is, her next address and phone number is...."

I dialed the number. No answer. Tired from the all-night, transatlantic flight, I checked into the hotel the man at the Houston flight club had recommended. I called home to say that I was safe in London. The girls reassured me they were fine: "Say 'hi' to Aunt Carolyn and Uncle Charlie."

I took a relaxed, soothing hot bath, dressed for an evening in London, and left the hotel. I boarded the red double-decker bus I had seen in all the iconic posters, and rode to Harrods. After shopping, I went to the theater to see Jeremy Brett and Edward Hardwicke as Sherlock Holmes and Dr. Watson. I felt good being on my own and confident that a good Sherlock Holmes mystery would provide some clues in finding my sister.

47. Sherlock

London

AFTER OBSERVING THE STRATEGY by which Dr. Watson and Sherlock Holmes scoured the environment, solved the mystery, and brought the action to a satisfactory conclusion, I exited the theater with new resolve to not spend a London weekend alone. Hailing a bulky black taxi, I climbed into a spacious back seat, handed the driver the address which went with the telephone number that did not answer. For the driver, it was an important clue. Within two blocks of the theater, the driver went slowly down a long row of brick townhouses that looked identical. At the end of the row, he took a sharp U-turn.

"Try that place up there. There is a call box on the outside of the door. Should be the number of the flat you want," he instructed.

"Okay, but please don't leave me here until I have made contact," I pleaded. "I can signal you if all is okay and if it really is my sister's place." I paid the driver before I stepped into the street. He observed my movements toward the call box.

Ring, Ring. Same ring sound as the phone in Sherlock's play. A male voice answered, "Hello?"

"Hello. Is this Charlie?"

"Yes, it is. Who might be asking?"

"It's Barbara! I've found you."

"Where are you?"

"At your front door."

164

I waved my thanks to the driver, and smiling, he drove on. I learned later how the conversation went on the other end of the call box when the ring occurred for the first time in their recently rented flat.

Ring, Ring.

Charlie: "I believe it might be the call box ringing,"

Carolyn: "How do you answer it?"

Charlie: "Hello? ... It's your sister."

Carolyn: "Where is she?"

Charlie: "On our front doorstep."

The front door opened into a medium sized living room, master bedroom, bath, kitchen, and small side bedroom with a hand sink in the corner. My sister rented this flat because of the side bedroom, anticipating the arrival at the end of the month of Audrey for her study-abroad program. The small bedroom would become my weekend retreat. Before I got too far into my story of why I was in London, I needed to retrieve my overnight bag from the hotel by Victoria Station.

My sister, brother-in-law, and I boarded the clean, efficient, and well-lighted underground Tube. It was late and dark as I began to unravel the story of Freddie 's previous weekend. After retrieving the overnight bag, we reboarded the Tube and returned to their rented flat in the theater district. Carolyn responded to my story:

"Interesting story. Did you know that our mother went on a shopping trip for a new fur coat when Daddy spent too much time in New York visiting his sister? I am not surprised you did the same thing. Tomorrow, after a good night's rest, we'll tour London, including Sherlock Holmes Museum and memorabilia shop."

Charlie teasingly added: "Knowing of your mother's fur coat purchase and, Barbara, your shopping spree and trip to London, I believe I will think twice before considering an extended trip without you, Carolyn."

In my trip to London, I needed to put distance over water and land between Freddie and me to get perspective of what has happened within my own home. I thought of Audrey's comments back in Richmond, how I denied comprehending the depth of her words. I thought of Suellen's revelation in "Everyone knows but you." I thought of the abuse of Ootah and me. With distance, the episodes were becoming clearer...real, undeniable.

On Tuesday, after the Martin Luther King, Jr. holiday, I flew home to Houston, and on Wednesday morning, I returned to work, having missed only one day, but a lot wiser and much more aware of the turbulence within my family.

48. The Couch

WHILE ATTENDING THE UNIVERSITY IN DALLAS, Suellen was seeing a therapist. I was asked by her therapist to make the four-hour drive to meet with him, and when I did, was told that my daughter wanted *me* to be in therapy. I asked for a recommendation of a therapist in Houston and was referred to Dr. Wunderman. I knew I needed help.

Dr. Wunderman listened quietly as I unraveled hurt and pain. After I finished venting, he asked. "What are you going to do about it? I looked at him in surprise. For forty-five minutes, I had poured out my heart. Dr. Wunderman listened without interruption. Now he asked a direct, simple, eight-word question. I was quiet, considering what he had just asked. I listened to the wisdom of silence permeating the room. Finally, from deep within, I heard my voice speak.

"I am going to write a letter to my daughters and tell them I believe their story of abuse." With the disclosure, I felt relief. I was going to do something. I would address the uncertainty.

"You have been a rug," Dr. Wunderman said, "allowing people to walk on you."

I thought about his image and smiled, visualizing the rug as a fine Persian carpet like the one Aladdin sat upon to fly over the city. My rug was finely knotted with deep rich red, cream, and blue colors. However, I was not sitting cross-legged, flying on top. I was hovered beneath the rug, studying the soles of those who walked on me. I began to laugh at seeing their soles and not their souls. I had a perspective that would have surprised the owners within the shoes. The more I considered the rug analogy, the more pleased I was with my visualization. I laughed. The laugh grew more intense and louder. Soon I heard Dr. Wunderman laugh, joining me in the joy of a secret discovery. I was slowly becoming more confident in who I was, opening the option of becoming single again, following a path where I would not be residing beneath a carpet. Within a few months, I was discussing plans of separation and divorce with Freddie. He pleaded, stalling for time. "Let us try to save this marriage. Let us go to a real marriage counselor."

"If you find someone suitable, I will consider," I responded. It was much too late to begin bartering, but I was willing to see whom he found that made an argument for sticking with him. When Freddie came up with a name, I submitted the choice to Dr. Wunderman.

"The therapist Freddie selected is not who he says he is; he is unqualified and not respected by my colleagues in practice."

Later, when I gave Freddie Dr. Wunderman's opinion, he responded. "Well then, you find a therapist you approve of."

I asked Dr. Wunderman. "What therapist would your professional colleagues see if they were in a similar situation as I am?" He considered the question and handed me a card for a Dr. Goldman, Psychoanalyst.

Somewhere within the Houston Medical labyrinth was Dr. Goldman's office. Freddie and I arrived separately, a few minutes ahead of the appointed hour. Both of us approached the office door and knocked. Dr. Goldman opened the door himself, and we walked directly into his office. It was a spacious room with low lighting, well-knotted Iranian rugs over a well-polished oak floor. Three brown leather armchairs, with a shaded floor lamp shedding a soft light, were waiting for occupancy. The temperature in the room was comfortable, not cool, and not hot, exactly right for calming an intense conversation. There was a soft leather couch at one side of the room, the kind one would see in a classy movie set of a high-end Freudian analyst. The total environment seemed on stage. The therapist wore a dark grey silk suit and shoes of smooth, thin Italian leather—stylish, expensive, and comfortable looking. The room décor spoke of someone making a handsome living. I settled into one of the armchairs and felt the cares of the world dissipating while I waited for the drama to unfold.

Dr. Goldman: "Who will begin?"

Freddie: "She has the list."

I had been conscientious in the task. Taking out my yellow pad, I began and talked steadily for half an hour, paused, and looked up.

Dr. Goldman turned to Freddie: "Your response to the charges?"

Freddie: "It's true. I suppose I will be going to therapy support groups every night of the week."

Dr. Goldman to me: "Why did you stay with him so long?"

Me: "That is why I am here, to figure it out."

Dr. Goldman spoke to us both: "Considering Freddie has addictions to lying, gambling, and sex, you must make decisions as to what comes next." The session ended.

Allowing Freddie to settle the tab, I rose from the leather chair and headed for the door, "addictions to lying, gambling, and sex" echoing in my brain. Dr. Goldman's psychoanalyst diagnosis gave me vocabulary to Freddie's behaviors that had nagged me. My public commitment "to honor in sickness and health" was altered. I opened the door to sunshine, held my head high, and knew my path would continue… elsewhere.

49. Dream Time: Here Lies Son of a Bitch

1990

I AWOKE WITH A STARTLE. Breathing hard, I looked around my bedroom with its familiar blinds, the window half open to let in the summer night air, the mirror on the wall. I knew where I was. It had been a dream. Strange. Voices spoke of a foggy history. I relaxed, let my head sink back into the pillow and allowed the dream to continue. Five women surround a casket and gaze with malice at the well-dressed stiff.

"Filho da Puta," says an attentive Black woman with a medium build, short-cropped curled hairdressed in a colorful full-flowing skirt, puffed-sleeve blouse, and brown leather sandals. "I was an immigrant from nordeste do Brasil. I was his empregada—his housekeeper, laundry woman, cook, plus all the 'extra' services he demanded. I needed income, and he took advantage of it."

"Son-of-a bitch" says a statuesque blonde, wearing a lab coat over her scrubs. "I met him when he came into the hospital with a heart attack. He was dead, but the attendants revived him. I have a large family in Northern Kentucky and with all his smartness, he was lonely and wanted family. We moved in together and had a son born at the same hospital."

"Son-of-a bitch" repeats an athletic, short, red-haired woman in brown oxfords, an earth mother type. "He told me his first wife was dead and his second wife was living the drug scene in California. I believed him. Among us middle-class folk, he gave the image of a successful businessman on the rise. It was when he picked up his three-year-old son from the nursery that I considered being the loving stepmother the kid needed. The man told me he needed dependents for a tax break."

"Hijo de quejarse," says the last voice raising her arms as if dancing a Flamenco. She was tall, well attired in a stylish red-print, wrap-around that highlighted her black hair and brown eyes. Her stylish high heels augmented her 5'10 height. "My late husband and I were merchants and had our own hacienda when Castro took over. Castro forced us out of Cuba. We immigrated to America. I was widowed when I met Freddie McMurray at a Methodist Church in Houston. He said he was an executive for an environmental engineering company. I had fiduciary responsibility and the management of North and South American holdings for a large estate. As a widow, I was looking for an intelligent and interesting date. When Freddie proposed, I thought my life would be fun and fill my lonely hours."

"Son-of-a-bitch," says a soft-spoken, attractive grandmother, a retired teacher. Widowed, I thought I had met a man who needed me. Told me he was lovely and missed his wife who died of cancer. I felt his loneliness, and I fell for his charm, stories, and beautiful Italian arias.

A bond of common stories and empathy among these five women was woven, securely, as if a shoelace were crisscrossed back and forth across the body. Looking up at each other, the women smiled in anticipation, appreciating what was yet to come. They chuckled and adjourned to the tavern next door.

Fully rested, I awake late the next morning, laughing, lying-in bed savoring the visuals of the dream. How many women in Freddie's life would show up for his funeral? Were the others so naive as I?

50. Leaving Town

BECAUSE I WAS FAITHFUL, I believed in his fidelity. I assumed Freddie's Methodist upbringing had provided him with guidelines for living. I trusted his intellect and business acumen. Fourteen years ago, I made a commitment before witnesses and in the sanctity of the church to love and cherish in sickness and in health. The vision of what I assumed to be the basis of a strong marriage did not exist.

Among the years, cracks appeared which I denied seeing. I did not question. I chose to believe only positive. I rationalized bad behavior. I ignored clues of impropriety. Bad became tangible. Cracks became fissures; fissures, crevices; crevices, an abyss. Fractures became hard to deny. As the marriage crumbled, I knew I had to flee, get out of town, away from the pain and confusion. I could not model a mother's behavior of remaining in an abusive marriage that was disrespectful to her and to her daughters. The model needed to change.

When I made the decision to leave Houston, I asked all three daughters, "Which direction should I travel? West, to where my sister and her husband lived on the water of Puget Sound? East, where Ken, family and friends lived?" Suellen was completing her junior year in college. She would be impacted as she was the only daughter to remain in Texas; yet she was on her way to independence. Audrey was enrolled for her freshman year at a college in Maine. Her father's sister lived there, and her aunt would be a family connection for holiday breaks. Emily still in grade school, was ready to move away from brokenness, so her opinion carried weight.

"Let's go to the Pacific Northwest," Emily said.

Audrey added, "If you return to Cincinnati, you are going home. If you go to Washington state, you will be starting over, not returning to your past."

The decision was made. The car would drive north and west. Emily and I would travel to the mountains where I had previously hiked, where I would be able to suck in fresh air to breathe and think. We could walk within old growth forests, connecting to the wisdom of time. We would learn to ski.

We sorted through the material stuff of our household. The home organ was given to our next-door neighbor to use in his school music program. The piano went to my health department colleague so her children could learn to play. A neighbor left computer boxes on the front porch. These were filled with household items and given away to various churches for their fundraisers. Emily's blue leather chaps, worn when she and her horse took first place at the regional horse show, would remain in Texas. The household items that were to move to a new state were packed into a moving van. Suellen and boyfriend would drive the van west, stopping in campgrounds for the night, removing chairs from the van to sit by the campfire, and weaving their way across Sierra Nevada mountains and along the Oregon Coast.

When the time came for Emily and me to depart, a small gathering of friends seated themselves on the green sculpted 1960s-era wall-to-wall carpet in the empty living room. I fetched the magnum bottle of Asti Spumante, once given to Freddie as a gift which I had successfully hidden. A bag full of MacDonald quarter pounders provided protein and energy. We feasted, drank, laughed, and told stories of our times together. When the bottle was empty, the hamburgers gone, and the stories shared, silence filled the room.

"Barbara, it is time for you to go," said my friend Nancy. These gathered friends urged me to sever the attachments to this Texas country home, get behind the steering wheel, and direct the car toward I-45, north to Dallas. Emily climbed into the front passenger seat. Waving goodbye, I slowly backed out of the driveway for the last time, noticing the hedge row I had planted, appreciating the waving bear grass with strong, white, fluffy-topped stems across the street, seeing how tall the Eastern pine trees in the backyard were that sheltered our home. I wondered if the black moccasin, who was there when we first arrived, would return to reclaim the back porch step.

Recalling eight years of Texas stories, we drove past the water tower park where Grandma Emilyna was retrieved by the police, past the utility park where Emily's horse had stepped on her foot, fracturing the media malleolus ankle bone, past the homes of good neighbors. When we reached the entrance of the subdivision, we turned left to Huffmeister, working our way to the Freeway. I was driving to a new state, a new job, a new home, and away from the man who had squandered fourteen precious years of our lives, my mother's inheritance, and put dents in my self-confidence. The new Honda would be paid for in time, but I needed it now for my escape. The car stayed on target, on a path away from Houston. Emily sang Girl Scout camp songs, while I focused on the drive. I was exhausted, numb, yet giddy with relief to be fleeing as we headed up the road toward a new start. The city of Houston could have this ex-husband.

51. Twenty-Two Years Later, Psych Class

Olympia 2012

I MOVED FROM TEXAS IN AUGUST OF 1990 and three months later Emily's father came to visit to tell us he would marry wife number four. Freddie returned to Houston and disappeared into the city of millions. Emily may have heard from her father a few times over the years, but he effectively disengaged from her life.

Twenty-two years after arriving in Olympia and having completed a Master of Science in Nursing from the University of Washington, I earned tenure as faculty professor teaching psychiatric nursing. Time, space, distance from Texas, and teaching mental health gave me a better understanding of the personality of Freddie McMurray. Specific diagnoses leaped from the psychiatric textbooks that seemed applicable: Impulsivity, Antisocial Personality Disorder, Attention Deficit, Narcissism. Dr. Goldman had diagnosed addictive behaviors to lying, gambling and sex.

I recalled Freddie McMurray's philosophy of life: "If I don't get caught, I am not guilty." Although it has taken these twenty years, I now have a clearer, textbook case of his behavior and personality. I have life experiences of stories to teach students to be sensitive for these symptoms of mental illness.

I prepared the class lecture on ten personality disorders. Deciding it would enhance student learning to act out each personality disorder, I copied and wrote scripts and engaged the college's drama department. Both the drama and nursing students studied the scripts. Class was scheduled to be held not in the nursing laboratory with technically programed mannequins, but in the Black Box, a small theater in the round within the Drama Department. Leaving the beds and mannikins behind, nursing students trekked across campus to watch drama students act out Ten Personality Disorders under a spotlight at stage center.

Nine scenarios were taken from a psychiatric text. I wrote the tenth scenario for antisocial personality disorder, experience gained from living with Freddie McMurray. This disorder is such a misnomer—in some ways, as to say "antisocial," you expect the person to display unlikeable traits. But, in realty, this person is the womanizer, the social butterfly, the gregarious, and popular charismatic person, the con man who pulls you into his center. I named the character in the antisocial personality disorder scenario "Tommy Jones," but the behaviors are Freddie McMurray. The student actor who took the role of Tommy Jones played the character perfectly. He nailed it. But how would the audience know how brilliantly the student actor played the part? Below is the script for Antisocial Behavior I wrote from experience living with Freddie McMurray.

Play Book Page 4: Cast of Characters - Ten Personality Disorders[2]

<u>301.7 Antisocial Personality Disorder</u>

Characteristic: "Patients with Antisocial Personality Disorder chronically disregard and violate the rights of others:" Some are engaging con artists; others, graceless thugs (Morrison, 474).[3]

Scenario: Tommy Jones

Under an alias, Tommy Jones managed to falsify his resume and con his way into respectable and responsible job positions which he held for a short period of up to five years. He finished high school, a program for the gifted. He had been caught three times for conduct disorder offences: bullying, extorting lunch money from a third grader, and finally getting a 17-year-old student pregnant. He stole books from the local library to advance his education. He was a womanizer, married, and divorced multiple times. He abused his stepdaughters and lied to his wife. He attended and had the children baptized in an upscale Methodist Church. His youngest was baptized in a Dior baby gown. He had the appearance of an upstanding member and wealthy contributor to the church. He tipped lavishly at restaurants, giving the impression of a rich patron, expecting service in return.

Role Play:

Confident, self-assured, smug, lying, and conning the class, Tommy Jones does a soliloquy to the students. He passes out chocolates with an attitude of superior intelligence, confidence, and arrogance:

Hi! I am Tommy Jones. I have had a good life – plenty of fun, games, pranks – always at the expense of others. But that is not my problem; it is theirs. Those people I took advantage of, well, they were ripe, available, and easily manipulated. My timing was right. And, you know if you are not caught, who is to say that you are guilty? Well, I shoplifted

2 Young, Barbara. Cast of Characteristics Playbook. Class lecture. Page 4,5. 2012.
3 Morrison, James. DSM-IV Made Easy: The Clinician's Guide to Diagnosis, Page 474-478. 1995.

and dealt in drugs. But ...I always got off. ...It's the skill of my operation. I am never at fault. It is always the other guy. I am smarter.

Got my education from Brooklyn Library. I used to throw books out the window and pick 'em up on the way home. Mom never knew; she was always working late at the distillery and thought that I, her son was an angel. I could do no wrong. Hey, I got my resume from the public library as well. You know, the place Ben Franklin started as a public service. It served me well. I have pulled the fake resume thing off many times. I look under "Who's Who" and copy their resume and take their name! Hell! I'm a good actor. Pull it off every time. Should get an Oscar for my performance.

My stepdaughters...well, I supposed I messed them up a bit, told them not to tell their mother. Their mother—she's naïve and unsuspecting. She believes I am her knight in shining armor. I conned her out of her mother's $25,000 inheritance. She still believes I am a prudent investor and will double that amount in no time. If she ever gets wise and begins to ask questions, I know where I can get another wife, ...at the church's divorced and singles group. It's the way I live...for the moment, on the run, and always covered by reputable people.

As the nursing and drama students were leaving the Black Box Theater, my hope was the audience and the actors were listening carefully and gained insight to the various personality disorders, especially, the well-acted antisocial personality disorder. I wanted the students to have confidence in themselves, to question those who demonstrate Tommy

Jones' characteristics. I wanted the students to protect themselves from unknowingly getting sucked into a relationship, getting conned as I had. I hope they would not accept, as I had thirty-six years before, the behavior of one I have come to call, "the Prince of Con."

52. Photographs – Prince of Con

Young Freddie is on the stoop in Brooklyn.

Freddie is the salesman ready to explain his idea for energy conservation.

Freddie, backyard chef. Enjoyed grilling brats

*Family photo taken with azalea bush in the garden,
Richmond, Virginia. Behind the smiles are different stories.*

*Wearing my sister's blue suit, selected by the wardrobe mistress, I was among five women
invited to Hollywood Studio 6 to tell our stories of being conned by husbands. The stories
promoted a detective's book on how to check out a potential mate before the con has a chance to
escalate. This event occurred several years after my divorce and escape from Texas.*

IV. Behind the Mask

1995-2020

FACIAL FEATURES WERE SHAPED,
paint applied and decorated with feathers
and beads. Stories emerged.

The Women of the Tribe

Convene the Circle

Invite me in

Teach me to construct the mask with strength

And paint it with a story from the heart

They place a medicine bag around my neck

Contains good medicine

Holds a crystal that I might see clearly

Into my hands, the women place a walking stick

To guide me on the path

The women of the Tribe

Release me from the Circle

Give permission to tell the story

Direct me to go out and

Share the healing powers of the mask.

53. Hidden Mystery or Life Story?

2017

A CONVERSATION WITH NAN

Barbara: Twenty-five years ago, Native women of a tribe on the bay taught me how to tell stories through the making of masks. Within the circle, artist Judith taught members of the women's group how to place plaster of Paris gauze strips on a partner's face to begin the structure of a mask. When the facial forms were dry, we painted the masks and attached whatever we wanted to embellish their beauty and uniqueness.

Nan: Masks scare me! I think they are trying to hide something I cannot see. I am uncomfortable and want to shy away from what you call a mask. Like Halloween, the mask hides the real you, and you are transformed into someone else. I can't get beyond my distrust of what I can't see. Masks do not speak the truth but cover for something else.

Barbara: The masks we built in the women's circle tell stories of pain, oppression, of children, journeys of failure and success, of love and loss. The stories are shared as we display the masks within a circle of friends.

Nan: What are you hiding that you are unable to tell me straight up? What do you keep protected? What are your losses of which you cannot let go? What is chained or hidden behind the mask?

Barbara: I don't know what it is I may be hiding. I want to dig deeper into my story and confront the losses. I'll start with birth order. I was the third child. My sister, five years older got along fabulously with people and was a well-spoken leader, an ease she might have taken into the political arena. As a kid my sister got up at 4:00 am to deliver the *Dayton Journal*

Herald. She wrote for her high school newsletter and in college studied journalism. She had the skills of success, and I studied how she make friends. As a towering figure in my life, my sister picked me up from kindergarten and walked me a mile home. To this day, she helps me with directions when I want to travel.

My brother was a newspaper carrier, an eagle scout, a thespian, debater, and basketball player. As kids, my mother gave us each a pair of boxing gloves, so we could duke it out. Brother was smart, too. He studied chemical engineering, became an investment consultant, and Civil War history buff. He could tell you the strategies of each regiment along both the North and South lines at Gettysburg. Never did I learn to be successful when debating my brother. He always had the arguments tightly crafted, and I stood wordless to compete. To this day, he is passionate about crosswords, pursing relentlessly all the letters into the boxes as he begins each day.

Being the youngest of three, I observed how my siblings coped with daily life. They showed me the way. I learned from the Presbyterian Church school that we were predestined. Therefore, I must have been programmed by birth order and predestined to be a mask maker. Behind the mask, the story of who I am could be revealed. The path I chose in life was neither my brother's nor my sister's, but I do acknowledge their giving me a head start.

Nan: My question remains. Who are you behind the mask?

54. At the Rez

1995

MY BOSS CALLED ME INTO HER OFFICE for consultation, indicated I had a problem, and referred me to the Employee Assistance Program (EAP) for employees with alcohol issues. I didn't drink. But I did take her referral and reported to the EAP. The counselor, after only five minutes into our session, referred me to the Career Transition Center. After a lengthy discussion, the Center referred me to my doctor. At my appointment the next morning, the doctor said: "You are experiencing Situational Anxiety. I will give you a prescription for two weeks medical leave of absence. You are to work every day to find a new job and you must exercise daily."

Following doctor's orders, I returned to the Career Transition Center to begin my search for a new job. The career counselor spotted a small ad in *The Olympian*. She said: "Barbara, here's a job for which you qualify. An Indian tribe on Willow Bay needs a program coordinator for a health grant. You will need to ask for an interview."

Two days later, I left Olympia for a two-hour drive heading west through the Black Hills in the direction of Aberdeen. I turned south at Monsanto past Mary's Lumber Mill where large logs were stacked in piles three times my height. The two-lane road curved like a serpent through the hills with no large condos, buildings, or shopping strips. I shared the road with logging trucks in a hurry to get to their weigh-in stations at ports in Aberdeen, Cosmopolis, and Olympia, unload, and return for more. When a logging truck was behind me, I looked for a turn-off space to let him pass. If I followed a loaded truck, I tried quickly to count the number of trees felled to make his load. I had trouble calculating an exponential number of trees leaving the forest, considering that I was on just one two-lane road at this hour of one day. How many trips were made during the day by the number of trucks hauling logs? How many felled logs added to the clear cut?

"This forest was clear cut in 1940 and replanted 1942." A billboard announced. Another read, "This forest was clear cut in 1990 and replanted 1995." I approached a flagger and stopped. A recent clear cut resulted in erosion to the main road. The crew was repairing the fallen roadbed, and I sat at attention until the flag person signaled me forward.

Approaching Raymond, I drove along the north side of the river to the bay, noticing fishing boats in the harbor. At this time of day, they were back from their morning catch. The drive continued through a small neighborhood to the edge of town where a sign alerted to fifteen more miles to the reservation. A short distance out of town, a farmer was moving cattle from one pasture across the road. I stopped the car and waited until the passage was complete, waved to the farmer, and proceeded on the road which hugged the rim of the bay.

Alone on the road, I noticed two dark human forms in high boots silhouetted against the sandy beach. Clam diggers with buckets and funnel tubes bent over their work, their feet sucked into the soft sand. A four-foot-high rocky levee separated the road from the beach and the tranquil waters of the bay. I took a deep breath, relaxed into the beauty of the natural vegetation, and enjoyed the solitude of the drive. The air smelled fresh and sweet. An Eagle flew overhead, circling. I took it as a good sign of what was to come. The next road sign read, "Entering the Cedar Bay

Indian Reservation." At the intersection, I turned and drove into the community.

Passing a small cul-de-sac neighborhood of equal lot sized HUD housing, I came to the tribal center on the inlet. A large sign announced, "Cedar Bay Tribal Community Center." A carving of Eagle with wings outstretched stood at the top of the sign. Turning into the parking lot, I got out of the car, stretched my legs, and looked around.

Across the road was the cemetery. Several plots had a small fence to encircle their family members. To the left of the parking lot was a trailer that housed the police and the tribal court. At the back of the Community Center was an ancient rotting dugout canoe, and behind the canoe the shoal waters of the bay. This was a spiritual place. I remembered as a teen being at church camp in the Ohio woods in morning meditation with these words, "Be still and know that I am God." Turning back to approach the front door, I entered.

As I waited for my appointment with the Tribal Chairman, I observed the lobby. A large display cabinet held Native-made baskets, several quite weathered, their designs faded. One door off the lobby was the entrance into the tribal clinic, dedicated in April, six months before my visit. Next to the front office, a wide doorway led into a branch of the Timberland Library. To the left of a stairway was a hallway hung with children's art. The hall led to the dining room and kitchen where senior lunches were served three times a week. To the left of the hallway was an entrance into the Meeting Room for health council meetings, tribal business, and ceremonial gatherings.

On its north wall of the Great Meeting Room hung a portrait of the ancestral chef, surrounded by smaller photos of tribal members. On the south wall was a large wood carving, "Watchers," by the tribal artist/archivist signifying connection to the ancestors. The tribal chairman walked into the room.

"Hello, Barbara, welcome. I am Chairman Joseph John. We will discuss the grant and your interest in this position. The work is this: Listen to the tribal women. Be sensitive to their grief and loss. Form a focus group with the women who have lost pregnancies. Develop a work plan to assist the women in accessing the same level of maternal healthcare enjoyed by white women in the Capital City.

The tribal women feel as though they are isolated. They often need to travel miles to maternity health care clinics and lack transportation. There are no private taxis and no county bus service to the reservation. When the tribal women attend local clinics, they feel misunderstood, and their cultural identity is not respected.

Congresswoman Unsoeld has taken this issue to Washington, D.C. and the Tribe has been assigned an advisory group composed of representatives of the Centers for Disease Control, the American Medical Association, University of Washington School of Medicine, Indian Health Service, The Cedar Bay Tribe, and the agency for Environmental Protection. The high rate of infant mortality at the reservation is unacceptable. With few live births, the tribe is in danger of extinction."

As Chairman Joseph John speaks, I think of the new markers I saw in the cemetery. We complete the interview and I begin the drive back to Olympia pondering what I have learned, using the two-hour drive to debrief. What were the reasons infant mortality on the reservation was at a higher rate than the white population that surrounds the tribe? Why were native women misunderstood at the doctor's office? Why were they treated differently, if treated at all? I wanted to return to the reservation to pursue answers to these questions. … Two days later, the chairman called:

I offer you the program coordinator job, but you cannot accept for three days. In that time, I want you to consider your commitment to the goals of the grant. If you accept the position, then you will stay for the length of the grant, three years. You may not accept the job, come, and then leave before the grant is completed, as so many before you have done. You will stay the length of the grant.

I thought about those conditions. Did I really want to make a commitment where, if the job did not suit, I could not leave? For three days, I waffled. Then, I called the chairman. "I will accept your position." … I gave my boss at the health department the required two weeks' notice and left at the end of the week.

AT THE RESERVATION, eight women of the tribe came forward to form the focus group to develop a work plan. They chose to start with grieving the loss of their infants and asked to create masks that would help them express their deeply guarded stories of pain. In making masks of their own portraiture, they would begin the healing process. I arranged for the meeting, and the women invited me to participate. We met the following Monday evening, turning the dining room into a mask-making workshop.

To start the evening, Midge, carrying an abalone shell with a smudge stick of sweet grass and sage, lit the stick, and wafted smoke in every corner of the room. Walking slowly, she chanted a prayer. Fragrant smoke of fresh herbs drifted lazily, temporally, in a light mist, eliminating any negative feelings which might have remained in the room from previous occupants and filling the room with a hint of healing salve. With the room prepared by the smudging ritual, ten tribal women entered and gathered in a circle. Rose began with a reading, author unknown, appropriate for the work we were to do:

"To discover who she is, a woman must descend into her own depths. She must leave the safe role of remaining a faithful daughter of the collectives around her and descend to her individual feeling values. It will be her task to experience pain…the pain of her own unique feeling, valued, calling to her, pressing to emerge. To discover who she is, a woman must trust the places of darkness where she can meet her own deepest nature and give it voice…weaving the threads of her life into a fabric to be named and given…sharing it with the women around her as she comes to a true and certain sense of herself."

Joann became my partner in constructing the mask on our faces. Each set of five women began, reverently, to dip the Plaster of Paris strips into bowls of warm water. Judith, our art teacher, instructed how to place the strips across the face in an "X" pattern to form an infrastructure of the mask construction. Additional strips went in a circular pattern from forehead to chin and around again to the forehead. Strips filled the empty spaces, leaving the eyes uncovered, or not, but the nostrils remained opened to breathe.

With my eyes closed, I sat still as a statue, while Joann dipped the fabric strips into the warm water and placed them on my face. Her touch felt like a gentle facial massage. The warmth was soothing and listening to the soft murmur of voices around me, I relaxed, letting anxiety slip way. I felt trust in Joann and a companionship with the other women. Yet construction of the mask created a barrier. I retreated, drifting further from the women and deeper into myself. I was searching, trying to find who I had become— divorced from husbands, a country away from the Ohio land of my birth, on an Indian reservation tucked into a cove of the Pacific Ocean, making masks with nine Native women. I will discover the self I seek to know.

It took only ten minutes for my face to be covered, and the warmth had given way to coolness. I was chilled and wanted the mask removed. Wrinkling my facial muscles into an angry mother lion in defense of her cubs, my three daughters, I snarled. The mask popped away from the anger, and in my hands lay my duplicate facial image. Placing additional Plaster of Paris strips around the edges of the mask as my mother would have placed seam binding on a new garment, l laid the mask aside to dry.

I became the mask architect of Joann's portraiture as she allowed me close to touch her face. I dipped the strips into warm water and started at Joann's forehead, making the X across the face, returning to the forehead to begin the circle, just as Judith had demonstrated, and as Joann had done for me. I filled in the open spaces. Joann was silent as I gently soothed the strips into place. As I progressed, Joann's nose took shape, then the curvature of her cheeks, the strength of her lips, and the shape of her jaw. I was seeing her features emerge as if for the first time to see her. Touching her face was intimate. Seeing her features emerge was sacred. I felt connected to her being.

When the warmth had dissipated, and the mask wanted release, Joanne roared. The mask dropped from her face. Holding it in her hands looking up to her, Joann smiled then laughed with pleasure. It was as if the mask spoke directly to her, "You are beautiful, and you are loved." Speaking to the mask, Joann replied, "You are beautiful."

After brushing a white gesso glue paint over the masks, we placed them in their starkness on a round table in the corner of the room. There they would dry and wait for next week's women's circle to take on paint and decorations, adding color and glitter to the story waiting to be told.

Same time. Same place. One week later...

The women and I retrieved the white masks, held them in our hands, studied them, and pondered how we would proceed. We gathered paints, brushes, water bowls, beads, feathers and began. Although there was a soft conversation around the table offering the support of community, each woman was in her own creative space. The circle gave each woman strength to speak through the mask.

We ended our evening with a talking circle. The stories that were released within the circle are forever the property of the storyteller. I was witness to an intimate sharing of deepest concerns. One mask had a key on the lips and a crystal tear falling from the eye. Another mask had a black hand covering the mouth for words she could not speak. Yet another mask grieved for nine children lost and rejoiced in five healthy grandchildren. Another spoke of the prayer and hunt for life.

When I was painting my mask, I allowed the inner voice to speak as if it were on automatic muse control. I chose the color, aqua, as it is pleasant contrast with my pale skin. Eyes were trimmed in white and then in red. Large "S" shaped squiggles of black, red, and yellow cover the cheeks. I painted a railroad track on the forehead. My nose looked like the beak of a bird, and my mouth was a yellow rectangle trimmed in red. I could not explain the squiggles, the beak nose, or the railroad and asked the women for their interpretation.

"Your eyes are open wide to learn but also sad," one said.

"There are question marks on your cheeks," said another.

"Your mouth is not natural. It has sharp corners, as if expressing pain, you cannot speak." said yet another.

It was difficult for me to speak; I was asking the mask to speak for me. Maybe the red around my eyes was my inside sadness, wanting to cry. … Later, I added stripped cedar, retrieved near my home in Olympia, from a logging truck going to the Port of Olympia. The cedar represented my Scottish auburn hair. The molted goose feathers I picked up at Capital Lake added a headdress. A former boyfriend David had given me a gift of earrings purchased a few years before at Vista House on the Columbia River. These earrings represented Spirit Quest. The necklace I made in the women's beading circle represents woman's heart, courage, and beauty. I was pleased with the overall artistic effect of my mask, and trusted that in time, the mask would release what it was I needed to know.

Speaks for me

55. At the Kitchen Table

1996

IN THE FIFTH YEAR SINCE LEAVING TEXAS, I became the host home to Jingyi, a Chinese Mandarin language teacher from Beijing, assigned to Emily's high school. At the time of Jingyi's home stay, I was employed at the reservation. Learning mask-making from the Native women, I wanted Emily, Jingyi, and me to make masks together, to transcend our painful life experiences to a space of healing and exploration. We began our work at the kitchen table. I lit a candle and placed it on the countertop to connect with the tribal women. When I was at the reservation and sat within the Native women's circle, I was moved into a sacred space, away from clutter, into affirmation and love. I wanted to bring the same feeling to the kitchen table.

Daughter Emily, a senior in high school and Jingyi, agreed to make masks. We were different ages, diverse cultures, and had our own life experiences. Emily had been born in Cincinnati, moved to Virginia, Texas, and Washington state by the time she was eleven. Like Professor Temple Grandin with Asperger's Syndrome, Emily loves science, math, and has a keen sense of animal behavior.

Jingyi was selected to teach advanced Chinese in Olympia, leaving her eighteen-year-old daughter and her husband in Beijing. Her family had suffered under the Cultural Revolution as Mao punished Jingyi's father for his critique of the revolution and sent Jingyi to the far north rice fields as a peasant laborer. As my guest, Jingyi was eager to participate in American life. We hiked in the Olympics, snowshoed at Mt. Rainier, and traveled the state. When I commuted to the Indian reservation for work during the week, Jingyi prepared Chinese cuisine for Emily. Her mask says this:

"I am the Yin and the Yang. I have been in the Cultural Revolution. I am here in the United States teaching. I suffered in the past. I am fortunate to teach and to see the world. Yin-Yang in Chinese philosophy are the two opposing principles in nature, the balance of life. If they are equal, life will be full of sunshine." Jingyi

I was upset with my communications with Emily. I thought she did not hear. When she was younger and we were living in Houston, I had her ears tested at the Blue Bird Circle Children's Hospital. As a teenager and computers were new, she spent focused time on her computer and did not speak to me. I felt cut off, ignored. When Emily left for Washington State University in Pullman across the state, I stared at her computer, thinking it the source of my non communication and distance from my daughter. I pulled the plug. picked up the computer, drove it to the dump, and gave it a hefty toss into the pit. I was tossing away, I thought, the disability to speak. It took Emily's mask to speak to me.

The eyes are open, painted dark with depth. She sees. Her ears are open flower petals. She hears. Tears flow down her face. She feels it all, including my anxiety when I did not understand. The lips are closed. Just as I was the third child, Emily is also the third child. Both of us found reasons not to speak. Emily's mask says: Sees everything. Hears everything. Feels everything. Says nothing."

At the reservation, I learned of the Medicine Wheel which teaches interconnection, and balance of physical, mental, emotional, and spiritual health. The Wheel represents the Circle of Life and has four directions: East is the birth, the beginning of the Circle, the rising of the sun, planting of seed, Spring. I painted this quadrant yellow. South represents youth, warmth, growth, and development, Summer. I painted it red, but I have seen this quadrant painted green. West represents adulthood, reflection, depth. The vastness and diversity of life is represented in black. The season is Fall. North is the whiteness of age, maturity, and wisdom. Winter. As we mature, we also continue around the Circle of Life where we become children again. The colors of yellow, red, black, and white represent the diversity of humankind.

In the center of my mask, I painted a tree. The trees in the Eastern woods sheltered my camping trips as a young Girl Scout. In the Pacific Northwest, hikes in the forest nourish my soul. I pinned a small orca whale in the dark waters of the West, remembering our kinship with the orca pods that migrate the Washington coast. Kinship with animals require us to keep our planet safe and habitable. Chief Seattle said, *"What happens to the creatures of our universe, happens to us."* I find tiny stones on the beach in colors of red, white, black, and yellow and attach them as trim.

When my art teacher saw the tree painted upon my mask, she noted that the tree was not grounded; it appeared a floating trunk. It did not occur to me to paint the roots. I allowed the tree representing my spirit to float. Now, whenever I draw or paint a tree, I show strong roots grounded within the earth, a network of communication gripping a diverse universe beneath the cover of soil.

Tree as Life Center by Barbara

Yin and the Yang by Jingyi

Sees Everything
Hears Everything
Feels Everything
Says Nothing
 by Emily

56. On Orcas Island

1997

SUZANNE, JO, AND I WALK onto the Washington state ferry docked in Anacortes, planning to join Edith at her home at Doe Bay on the far side of Orcas in the San Juan Islands. After walking aboard and finding seats, we lean over the railing, and watch as traffic engineers load cars, service trucks, campers, and bicyclists into the lower deck, snuggly fitting them in and balancing the weight. With a long toot signaling departure and a strong turbulent thrust against the pilings, we set sail. Departing Anacortes, we sail first to Lopez and Shaw Islands before arriving at Orcas. I wrap my jacket tightly around me as I stand on the open deck, letting the wind blow my hair any way it wants to go. I grip the rail for stability, gaze into the waters being pushed aside by the boat's prow, and image myself on a mighty adventure that only I could take by not hesitating to step forward into the day. I let the captain chart the passage and I let go of concerns, enjoying the freedom that comes from leaving the port and heading toward whatever is to be.

Scheduled stops at Lopez and Shaw discharge and take on passengers fitting into space available. Upon reaching Orcas, the captain glides through the guide pilings and maneuvers a snug connection. Thick rubber fenders bounce the ferry gently until the boat settles calmly into the groove. Thick ropes are passed between the workers, and the ferry is securely tethered to posts. The gangplank is lowered, and the discharge begins. Cars and trucks quickly depart, and head left up the hill toward the village of Eastsound. Cars on the right side start their engines and wait for the signal to replace the departing cargo. We disembark the walk-off passenger ramp to firm ground and Edith's greeting.

Suzanne, Jo, and I climb into Edith's car, and we all head up the hill toward Eastsound. We pass through the town, on through Marin State Park, past coops and vineyards, vegetable gardens, and modest homes of those who live off the land. We ride past young people kayaking in the inlet, past Rosario Resort, and to the far side of the island where Edith's home sits on a bank that slops to the inlet. Edith tells us the story that one night she was awakened by the chattering sound of an orca pod returning to feed. Edith put on her robe and shoes, walked down the bank in the dark, sat and listened as if she were eves dropping a family discussion. *"Beautiful music, this conversation,"* she said. *"I was invited into their family circle, a guest of the pod."* Edith spent the rest of the night sitting on the hill, listening.

Edith's kitchen is our workspace for mask making. We cut the strips, build the structure on our partner's face, and remove the masks to let them dry. We place them in a low heat oven to hasten drying. Then, leave the masks on a rack on the countertop and drive to town to look for garage sale trinkets to decorate. Edith finds a maroon pompom to use for hair, and she mimes being a show girl. Suzanne's mask's vivid coloring mirrors her active life. Jo adds a whistle to hang around the neck of her mask, as she is the matriarch of her family.

My mask is the tartan of the McGregor Clan, symbol of my father's Scottish heritage. In 1993, daughter Audrey took her junior college year abroad at the University of Glasgow. Visiting her there, we toured Northern Scotland and the Isle of Skye, visiting the Battle of Culloden where Bonnie Prince Charlie and his clan men fought the English. Walking the paths of the battlefield, I felt the spirits of those who fought and died there. Bonnie Prince Charlie and his tired clansmen were defeated, lost their clan identity, and remained forever under the rule of England. Walking the battlefield, I was connected to my Scottish ancestors.

I remembered the lecture of Professor Joseph Stone in graduate school at the University of Washington in my course on Native culture and mental health nursing. Dr. Stone, a member of the White Springs Tribe of Northern Oregon, discussed the pain of loss that is carried by Native generations, descendants of Wounded Knee. A sad history of women, children, elders, and medicine people massacred by the U. S. Cavalry that wanted native people removed from the land. *"Grief passes through the generations,"* Dr. Stone said. He drew a family tree upon the board and showed the descendants who survived the massacres could be the patients who come to our mental health clinics with depression, anxiety, and addiction.

Día de Los Muertos is a Hispanic commemoration of the ancestors who have passed on. The beloved ancestors are invited back to take food and drink and dance with their living descendants. A place is set for them at the table. Last year, on the second anniversary of Ken, my first husband's death, a place was set for him at the table. My granddaughter went to the garage refrigerator to fetch a Dr. Pepper, her grandfather's favorite drink. Around the table, we told stories as his portrait gazed down upon the empty chair.

At an August Olympia Bon Odori festival, the Japanese ancestors come back to dance in the streets with their living descendants. The dances portray the life of fishermen pulling in their nets and the rigors of mining, shoveling coal. Olympia's diverse community joins in the dances as the songs are played on loudspeakers and Taiko drummers beat the step. The songs direct our movements of casting fishing poles and reeling in the catch. Dancers shovel the coal and throw it over their shoulders. The circle of dances continues until all the stories have been told. As the evening progresses and day becomes night, we set lighted candles on small sailboats and place the boats into Capital Lake. The current sails the boats across the water, lighting the path for the ancestors to return home.

Painted upon my mask is the McGregor Plaid. In the strength of my father's faith of Presbyterianism is the doctrine of predestination which, as a child, I never understood. Was my being a nurse pre-destined? Was it predestined I feel spirit of the ancestors and sorrow on the Battlefield of Culloden?

My brother Jerry is the historian in our family. He told me of his visiting Andersonville Prison several years ago where a few of our ancestors on my mother's side died as prisoners in the Civil War. Because there was little food and poor sanitation, prisoners died of malnutrition and disease. Jerry encouraged me not to visit the battlefield, as I would feel what he did, the pain and suffering of ancestors who died there.

Our society is recognizing the intensity of Black Lives Matter. Stories are shared of pain and loss of black enslaved peoples who helped build the country's economy by their work in the cotton and tobacco fields and on the railroads. The message of injustice has taken to our streets in cities across the nation.

We are unmasking the pain of our ancestors. Our masks will help us connect and understand the depth of our losses.

McGregor Clan

57. Making Masks at a Scientific Conference

1998

AS A MEMBER of the Public Health Nursing Section and the Native American, Alaskan Native, and Hawaiian Native Caucus, I submitted a proposal for a session in mask making at the Annual Meeting of the American Public Health Association. My proposal was accepted into the conference program.

There is magic in the process of making masks. "Magic" because I cannot explain it. It is science too, involving the brain, memory, and emotions. As expressed in the native medicine wheel, it is the connection of spiritual, emotional, physical, and mental. The medicine wheel is a healing circle. I made masks at the Indian reservation; took the practice home; and shared it with nursing friends on a retreat in the San Juan Islands. Now, I present mask making at a professional international meeting which I attend each year to get grounded, enhancing my work in public health nursing.

Offered in the evening after a long day of scientific presentations, lectures, and poster sessions, twenty people came to my session, ready to learn what is behind the making of masks that will enhance their work in healthcare. I introduce a two-evening program. In the first session, we make masks, using our own faces as models. The second session to be held the following evening at the same late hour, we paint the masks and tell our stories.

Conference participants engage. Tired from a long day of professional presentations, they let down their business façade, relax, listen, become partners, and make masks. I become animated, forgetting that I do not normally engage as a loquacious speaker. I jettison into a transforming space beyond words, allowing the spirit of connection to permeate the session.

A slender, tall young man stretches his legs out from a sitting position in a chair, resting his head against the back so that his diminutive elder lady partner can reach him. Strips of plaster of Paris gauze are cut and ready to apply. Small, wrinkled hands reach out to touch the young man's face. Over a thin coating of Vaseline, the elder lady applies the gauze strips to his face. The young man sits in silence, feels the warm touch, and fades away into his own thoughts. For ten minutes the young man sits without stirring, listening to a recording of the native flute of R. Carlos Nakia, and a background of soft tones of many voices. The gentle sounds blend into harmony. The masks slowly, one by one, are removed from partners' faces. There is wonderment of the creation they hold in their hands.

"Oh, its' beautiful!" I never would have thought …"

"I had no idea I could see my own image as I have done tonight."

"Amazing! I am calmed by trust in a perfect stranger," the Elder says as she laughs and looks up into the eyes of her tall partner, "I don't even know your name!"

The partners switch roles, and the architect becomes the model. Construction of masks is reciprocal. When all partners are finished, the masks rest. Tucked safely away, the masks will return for the second session the following evening. Their stories will then come into the circle to be told.

When I facilitate a mask making seminar, I rise above the everyday existence of survival, as if a ray of sunshine is gleaming directly on my head and surrounds me in a mist of love. A feeling of safety encourages me to be myself, to speak. I lead the session with an infused energy. I feel connection with the native women who taught me this practice. I accept the energy given to me. The masks will reveal tomorrow what it is we are to share.

Bringing their unpainted masks, participants return the next evening. Sitting at tables, they choose brushes and reach for small acrylic paint bottles. Artists chat softly while focused on painting. When the masks are ready to present, the participants form a circle, and pass a talking stick, allowing the one who holds the stick to speak while others in the circle listen. Stories of mothers, illness, partners enter the circle. Stories of love, sorrow, joy, and tears are relinquished to the circle. Tales from the heart touch the hearts of others.

The next day, participants will return to sessions concerning global health disparities having, the night before, allowed themselves to hear and to tell the stories behind the masks.

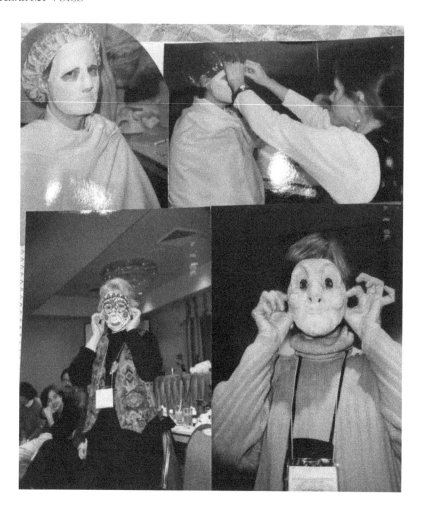

"Healing through Masks: An Ancient Tradition of Storytelling," offered by Public Health Nursing section, American Public Health Association Annual Meeting. Washington, D.C.

58. Behind the Ropes

2006

THE PSYCHOLOGIST RESPONDS to the photo I bring to the therapy session of a mask bound in rope. She says, "This photo speaks of someone who is tied up, caught behind a lattice cross-hatched fence, shrinking from boldness. Reminds me of the eyes of immigrant children at the Texas border, held captive, looking through the chain fence. The face beneath these ropes may want to speak but is bound in silence."

Her comments punch me in the gut. The framed photo I gave the therapist was of my latest sculpture—a painted facial mask to which I added a weaving of seagrass rope, like the mesh helmet used by a fencer. Mine was not a tight screen as in a fencer's helmet, but a loose open weave that I practiced in basket class. The therapy sessions analyze my art, and the sessions go like this: I carry a piece of my artwork to the session. The therapist describes how the art affects her. I ponder her comments, and if I can respond at the time, I do. Most often, I sit in silence, and think about what she says and how the mask speaks to her. This time, however, the therapist's comments, "being tied up and hiding behind a mask," is particularly sensitive. The mask behind which I am hiding is there to protect me. Or she could be right. I am tied up, trapped. I consider what she said and comment.

"I really don't know why I made it that way. I start an art mask because I want to speak but I don't know what I want to say or how to say it and let the mask portray what I need to say. I leave it to the muse."

My therapist is a PhD psychology student intern. This is her last quarter of study before graduating to professional practice, and she must have a certain number of student practicum hours to graduate. It is my last quarter too, to receive a master's degree in nursing education, and I am looking forward to teaching. The psychology student and I take advantage of each other.

2020

Fourteen years since I graduated with my master's degree, I am isolated in a different way. COVID. At seventy-eight, I am at risk for the virus. I have come to know the contours of my home, enjoy cooking a nutritious meal, and often light a candle to dine with myself. Zelda, my cat, joins me at her kibble dish on the floor. On a climb up the steps to the attic to open the vents for spring, daughter Emily noticed scattered insulation, and she surmises rodents, squirrels, over the winter months, have found holes to enter and have recycled insulation into soft nesting material. I survey the mess, call, and contract new insulation installation. Before the lockdown in March, a team of workers come to replace the insulation. I clear the attic of storage boxes.

I am curious what I have stored in the boxes, wondering what was so important I tucked away all these years. The outside of one box is irreparably damaged, the side having a large chewed away hole. Tooth marks are evident. Sawdust, or the bits and pieces of discarded cardboard lay around the box. After removing a chewed foam pad covering the box contents, I remove the Behind the Ropes mask. The face of the mask is painted in a soft grey tone, much like the skin color of Amy Sherald's portrait of First Lady Michelle Obama now hanging in the National Portrait Gallery in Washington, D.C. The mask face is cleared of rope, removed from the forehead to the chin. The grey-brown nose has been chewed leaving a hole. The red lips have been chewed, leaving another hole, but it is the absence of the rope from the eyes, cheeks, and mouth, allowing the mask to come into existence, which fascinates me. The rodents have carted away the rope fibers leaving the mask exposed, open to speak, to tell a story. I laugh at the cleverness of the rodents recycling nesting materials, liberating the mask from behind the seagrass rope. I am delighted in its emergence. I wonder what the psychologist would say.

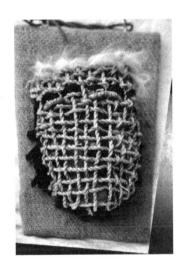
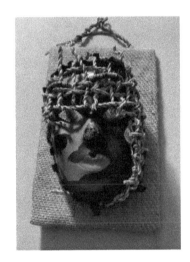

59. Kintsugi[4]

2010

"GOODBYE." The nursing student gently moves the fingers of her raised right hand so the young woman patient on the other side of a small window of the heavy locked door could see her wave. Their eyes meet, conveying concern, caring, puzzlement of the lives they live that erects a door on the ward of a mental hospital to come between what in the world outside the hospital could be a friendship. I am a nursing instructor witnessing this exchange. The student, troubled and deep in thought, reports to our end-of-shift debriefing session of clinical practice. When her peers gather and I open the discussion, the student blurts out her concern:

"You know, we are the healthy ones who can leave this place and walk into the sunshine. The woman I said goodbye to is my age and is my patient care study. Her name is Carol. She must stay here and live behind the locked door until she is ready to cope with the culture outside the hospital walls. She and I are not much different on either side of the door. I could be she. She could be me. It is a fine line that pushes us one way or the other...toward health or into depression. Carol is so much like me, and yet not. She tried to commit suicide by lying on the railroad track. Now, she copes with her depression and the loss of a leg."

The wave at the door window seemed so simple a gesture and yet a powerful message—a caring, a connection from one young woman to another, similar in age, and beauty, and desire to be seen and heard.

---

[4] Kintsugi, "a centuries old Japanese method of repairing pottery with golden paint. Also called 'golden joinery.' By repairing broken ceramics, it is possible to give a new lease of life to pottery that becomes even more refined thanks to its 'scars.' The Japanese art of kintsugi teaches that broken objects are not something to hide but to display with pride." (Wikipedia)

Instructing in psychiatric nursing practice at the community college, I needed some down time and chose to be absorbed into a class of young student artists within the ceramic's studio. Large blocks of clay are delivered to the ceramic studio for student use. Pinching off a mound of clay from the hefty block, I work it with my fingers. Throwing the clay body on the canvas covered table, I pound, press, hit it with my fist, fold it over as if I am working with bread dough, and press again. It feels good to manipulate the clay in my hands as though I have been given exercises from the physical therapist for strengthening hands and fingers. I press the clay into a shape with an idea in mind. Or is the clay in charge of how it is to be shaped? The mind, the fingers, and the clay piece become a creative team.

Remembering what I had witnessed in the facial expressions between two women on opposite sides of a locked door, I press the ball into a flat slab. The slab becomes an oval and slightly concave. Eyes are cut into the slab. I use slip, a muddy clay, to massage the clay piece, a process known as burnishing. Becoming momentarily distracted from the burnishing, I press too hard, and the clay piece breaks into two pieces. I apologize for not giving the piece my full attention and continue the massage with the two pieces, this time with total attention and gentler strokes.

The ceramic students plan to take their clay pieces to the country. A farmer has agreed to our digging a fire pit on his property. The pit will become an earthen kiln and we will tuck our clay pieces into the pit to bake and harden. The kiln will burn during the night, and the next morning, we will retrieve our pieces from an exhausted kiln.

Purposefully, we dig the pit. We place our clay pieces. Covering all the art with paper, sticks, saw dust, heavier logs, we bid our clay pieces a safe journey. We set a bonfire and when we are sure the kiln is under control and steady, we cover with a corrugated roof. One of our groups is on night guard duty. Classmates will return to retrieve the pieces in the morning.

In returning, I see my classmates lift their pieces from the pit, marveling at the variance of how each piece was fired, depending upon its placement in the kiln in relationship to the heat. My professor does not see one of my pieces among the ashes and accidently steps on it, breaking it in two. I have now three pieces of a fired clay mask of black patches on pink, pink being the areas I burnished. The night firing determined the design, and it is earthy and beautiful.

Back in the ceramic studio, I break the three pieces into seven, a sacred number. What is broken, can be repaired. The Japanese practice of Kintsugi brings broken pottery pieces together with gold paint, calling it "golden joinery," revealing and emphasizing the cracks and enhancing its total beauty and strength.

The gentle wave of a nursing student to her care study is the golden joinery to make the broken whole again. I feel as though the broken pieces of my past are coming together with golden glue creating the joinery, making the broken whole.

Seven broken pieces become a whole facial mask.
It was left unrepaired and not submitted to Kintsugi.

The repair of this broken mask was done by golden joinery, the Japanese practice of Kintsugi.

60. Onion Skins Peeling

2011

PULLING MY MASK ART FROM THE STORAGE CLOSET where it has been hiding for years, I notice how sad the figure looks and with onion skins cascading from the face down the front of a feminine jacket, long since out of style. The facial mask is two identical masks. The one in front is separated into two pieces and opens to the inner mask. I set the jacket and mask set aside.

I fetch a hoe from the shed and cultivate a small patch of flower bed on the east and sunny side of the house next to the alley. My sister separated her iris rhizomes and brought me a dishpan full. I wanted the earth to receive these rhizomes, give them nourishment in a new home and next summer bloom in purple glory for the neighbors who use the alley as a walking path. It felt good to have the hoe in my hands. I felt in touch with my ancestors who were farmers. Mom always said, "Our ancestors were among the first pioneers into the Ohio Territory and farmed the land." I want to know these ancestors and understand our beginnings. As if peeling away the onion skins layer by layer, I want to know my family's core.

Rev. James Finney set up his church north of Pittsburg near the Monongahela River in 1768. His son, John Finney, went east at age fifteen to be a drummer boy in the Revolution and an aide-de-camp to George Washington. For his military service, John was granted land in Ohio. This land grant deposited my lineage in Ohio. My brother, Jerry, is the historian in the family and tells of one story of an ancestor who floated the family possessions down the Ohio River to settle in southern Ohio. Not sure that this is fact or legend, but it adds to the family lore. As a child, I enjoyed visiting my grandparents who lived in southern Ohio, in the town of Waverly, located halfway between Chillicothe, the first capital of Ohio, and Portsmouth on the Ohio River. I was told that this was good fertile farming country – Pike County. My grandparents moved from the farm into town so that my mother could attend high school. On the edge of Waverly town is Union Cemetery where my ancestors are buried. My beloved grandfather James Rufus Finney and Grandmother Josephine Marks Finney whom I visited as a child in Waverly and who lived their last years with my mother in Dayton are in Union Cemetery. Great Grandfather Walter Finney and his wife Harriet James Finney are buried at Union. Great grandfather Andrew Finney and his wife Lucy Merrill Finney are next to Walter and Harriet. As a child rubbing with charcoal on tracing paper the names of these ancestors, I was reaching to touch my heritage. In recent years, Uncle Harold Aldon Finney, my mother's brother, who lived to be one hundred, is buried at Union. The only living relative in Waverly today is my first cousin John Finney.

Mom worked for years on paperwork to show that she was a descendant from John Finney who served in the American Revolution. When I was in high school in Dayton, I took off from school one day to gather with family members and the DAR (Daughters of the American Revolution) to dedicate a monument to this John Finney at the site in Newcomerstown, Ohio. It was an important event for my mother. Her family was documented to the beginning of the Republic.

Thank you, facial mask from the closet, for peeling away the layers that have covered us for two centuries.

In remembering my ancestors, I now lay the iris rhizomes in the dirt and encourage the roots to reach into fertile soil.

61. Transition Mask

1996

THE TRIBE WAS CELEBRATING its annual sobriety pow wow with invited dancers, fresh hot fry bread, with salmon, elk, deer, oysters, and berries on the buffet. There was drumming and singing. I sat in the grandstand when not on duty at the buffet table and watched with awe the beautiful movements of the Tlingit fancy dancer, alone on the floor. The dancer was a strong tall man wearing a heavy carved cedar mask of Raven that transformed him into the bird. He pulled strings that opened and closed the beak in speaking his story. He raised Raven's head and lowered it, looked right and then left as he moved around the dance floor, the gymnasium of the local school. Raven's long arms were covered in a coat of feathers and the dancer bird moved his arms up and down as if he were flying. Raven moved in grace and strength as he engaged us with his dance.

A group of five drummers circled a large central drum, beating rhythmically, powerfully, and singing. Singers and Raven were in harmony, the beat of the drum with the step of Raven's feet. I was lifted from my bleacher seat into Raven's story, mesmerized with the drumming and Raven's movements across the floor. I felt transformed.

2007

In a ceramic shop on campus, I work the clay with my hands, slapping out air bubbles and pressing with rollers a large flat slab. I shape eyes, nose, ears, mouth into a facial figure. The clay feels flexible in my hands; fingers agile, as I create a humanoid likeness. From the discarded, unwanted bin of to-be-recycled clay pieces, I retrieve a tiny face, the creation of another, that I place on the forehead of my figure like a third eye, the muse, or the ancestors, who continue to inform and influence my life.

After bisque firing, I chose the colors for glazing. The face color is a glossy pink. The eyes are deep navy blue, almost black rimmed in royal blue. White teeth are exposed with thin blue lips shaped, not in a smile, but a strained tension. The partner mask begins as a facial structure on a flat narrow slab of clay having been pounded and rolled to flatness. Eyes and mouth are convex coiled clay circles. The nose becomes a protruded beak. Texturing is roughed with a blunt carving tool, representing feathers. I slice the clay face into two equal sides. In glazing, the figure is black, and the eyes and mouth, unglazed and remain the natural color of the clay.

My brother-in-law, Charlie, has a fully equipped workshop in the basement of his home on Budd Inlet. I carry the two partner ceramic pieces to his basement to build a wooden structure that will connect the pieces as a transition mask. I do not intend to dance the mask, but I do want to express an ability to transform. Measuring, sawing, hammering, painting, Charlie and I build the structure. The humanoid is framed in a black box. The beaked bird has hinges attaching it to the front of the box with dowel rods to facilitate movement of the transition. The bird becomes the door to open and close the view to the pink face. The two are engaged in transformation.

2020

The Transition Mask hangs on my wall, reminding me of daily transition. The mask I wear today is a facial mask to protect others and me from transmission of the COVID virus. The same mask also gives modest protection from the air I breathe, today rated as, "moderate unhealthy" by air quality standards. Wildfires are burning in Northern California, Oregon, and in Washington. Charlie sold his home on the Inlet and has moved to a retirement community where he now resides in the Gentle Care Unit. I am isolated in my home, writing mask stories, looking forward to the day when I can sit with family for dinner. Transition occurs daily.

Transition Mask

62. Within the Cartoons, Characters Speak Truth

2016, 2020

CARTOON CHARACTERS IN THE DAILY PAPER provide personal essays that target truth in politics, and with a few strokes of the pen, the political cartoonist interprets the state of the Union. I begin my day with the "funnies" to understand the tension in our country. Pig, rat, goat, cat, dog, and Pooch are among my daily reads. In the strip, "Family Circus," children run around the neighborhood, in and out of backyards, over fences, around houses to discover whatever they need to know about the environment. In another strip, an elderly couple who see and hear through diminishing facility, answer their grandson's questions of life. Snoopy returns to his typewriter on top the doghouse to work on his novel and to discuss with Woodstock, a small yellow bird, the politics of home. These cartoon characters speak truth through their simple and direct dialogues.

Sometimes Mr. Trump. seems like a cartoon character except he doesn't have as much awareness or interest in exploring his environment as do the children and animals. He takes himself much too seriously and seldom if ever laughs. His work tends to divide instead of bringing us together to enjoy and laugh at the complexities of life. The animals can interrupt, through their creators, the political talk of the day. Yet, I don't know how to interrupt the ramblings of Mr. Trump. which are scary, frightening, self-centered, and totally lacking in compassion.

The day after the presidential election November 9, 2016, I wrote a poem and read it the same evening to the gathered writing students at the coffee shop Traditions. My poem is not a cartoon but serious. I say this:

Let me be accepting...as

The political vote

Did not go in my favor

Let the new leader learn to compromise

Soften his tongue

With those of different faces

Let me recommit to those values

That made our country

The hope of those who came searching

Let me roll up my sleeves

Retreat to a quiet room

Use my pen to speak truth

Let me love with confidence

Dance for freedom

Sing with harmony

Live life I have been given

I express my disconnect with Mr. Trump through my ceramic mask. Because he lost the election, this actor president will be leaving his stage, the White House, next month—his role tarnished. His is no longer a silly, sad cartoon, but a character in a tragic play. The animals in the cartoon strips continue to discuss wisely how to live with COVID, how to relate to their neighbors, and find balance in life. Their guidance is worth reading. They speak truth.

Hair Piece

61. Depois Da Hora Do Urubu

(After the Hour of the Vulture)

2021

IN WRITING CLASS, I composed this fictional story of a nurse named Cassy, taking the risk of stepping into the darkness. This chapter relates to the memoir year of 1966-68 in Chapter 23, where I regretted not stepping into the night to discover the source of hypnotizing rhythm. Through the fictional writing, I explored what Cassy discovered that sultry night fifty-four years ago.

The evening *passeios* of arm-in-arm young women parading by the young men hanging out in the *parque* watching the young women, have ended. The vulture has completed her circling, looking for dinner. The guitars have been put away. The town has bedded for the night, and children are falling asleep. A single light bulb hanging from the wood rafter in the main room of simple homes burns brighter against the darkening night. With long auburn hair, Cassy stands in the frame of the back door of her clay-floored home, alone, looking out beyond the well to the backyard garden. The well is now silent from the day's gossip of neighbors around its rim. Evening is settling from an active day. The night is quiet. Except...

Ever so faintly, Cassy hears distant chanting, reminiscent of a religious service, yet different from the organ Bach cantata she would hear at home. A small gentle wave of the day's released heat wafts across the dark, bringing in its mist, the enchanting rhythm. She listens intently as if the beat is coordinating with her heart and is calling to her through the darkness of the night. She hears it signaling, as a beacon to come, join the song, and dance to the enticing beat.

Stepping forward into the night in the direction of the sound, Cassy leaves the security of her home and her Midwestern caution for whatever lies before her. As if a rope is wrapped around her waist, she is tethered to a source, pulling her toward the sound in the night. With just enough light to illuminate her steps and keep her from stumbling, she follows the road by the light shining around the cracks of doors and windows of houses huddled close to each other and just a step off her path. Her pace unites with drumbeats. She is tugged forward into the darkness.

Cassy was not aware of how far she walked when she reaches a large meeting house on the edge of the *sertão*, the scrubby backland. On the front door is a carved wooden mask of *Oxací*, the God of Travel. She shudders, feels chills over her body even though the night is hot. The beat in her brain urges her to grab the handle, take the risk and discover what is on the other side of the door. Shaking, her hand pushes against the door, opening to movement, music, song, and dance. She quickly slides onto a bench in the back of the room and acclimates her senses to the scene, getting her bearings, and trying to blend even though her skin color is pale compared to theirs.

Two bare-chested men in rolled-up pant legs are engaged in an athletic dance doing cartwheels toward each other as if wanting to kick a foot to the head of the other, then backing off, not touching, but threatening. She is witnessing an ancient dance of *capoeira*, amazed at the men's athleticism and energy. Sweating and exhausted, the men retreat.

Dressed in white billowing dresses that almost scrape the dirt floor, black-skinned women's bare feet tap the ground with the same beat as the drum. Like waves of the ocean, the women undulate, stretching their bodies erect, heads held high and eyes looking to the thatched roof. The pose holds for only a second and the women bend low, as if trying to touch their heads to the floor. A chorus of voices matches the undulations, adding to the cacophony.

Entrancing music focuses Cassy's attention on the band. Several men in short-sleeved shirts and khaki shorts, with their toes in flip-flops, create the sound that drew her to this place. Two drummers beat on cone-shaped drums and one man plays the bottom of a large metal oil can. Three more men form a string section, strumming the berimbau which blends a twangy pluck. With a small metal stick, another man clanks against a metal double horn-shaped instrument. Metal against metal adds a two-toned tinny accompaniment.

These musicians and these dancers are descendants of their enslaved ancestors who came from Africa to work in fields of sugar cane in Bahia on Brazil's eastern coast. The sounds they make come from their souls and are part of their DNA. Arms of the drummers and faces of the undulating dancers glisten with sweat.

A hand reaches over to Cassy and offers her a smoke, an invitation to join the celebration and move from spectator to participant. She takes a deep puff, passes it back, and lets her muscles and attitude relax. The hand returns, offering a cup. She accepts and drinks of an unknown juice called *juremí*. Cassy is no longer chilled. She has eased into the environment. Her bones absorb the music. She feels the twang of the berimbau, the beat of the drums, and the urge to join the dancing. She is intoxicated.

The *Mãe de Santo* (Mother of Saints) begins to shout, swirl, shake, screaming words from a forgotten language – "*Eminotim vê, É, ê, ê, Andó xó cá ê vô a, A, a!* Her eyes roll back. She is in a trance, possessed, connecting with the Spirits. Dancers back away and give her the space to undulate. After a few minutes of possession, the *Mãe de Santo* crumbles to the ground, exhausted. Dancers assist her from the floor and attend to her as others catch the spirit, shaking and shouting.

Having drunk from the cup, Cassey rises from the bench and moves forward into the dancing. She is now the one undulating, swaying back and forth, swinging side to side, singing, *"Eu sou Amerinho. Su sou vista pena. Eu sou vim en terra para beber juremí."* (I am a little American. I only wear feathers. I come down to earth to drink juremí.) Cassy shouts and shakes, sweats, and glistens. She is possessed by the Spirits. After a while, her muscles relax, and she falls to the hard-packed ground.

Cassy, the young Peace Corps volunteer from the heartland, reared in the Gothic Presbyterian Church, the dedicated nurse who once wore a starched white nurse's cap laundered to cardboard stiffness by the Chinese laundry, tonight let go of her proper persona, joins the Spirits in dance, and experiences ecstasy. Tonight, Cassey became a part of the community she came to serve. No longer is her name *Dona Americana* or *Dona Branco*. She is now affectionately *Minha Neguinha*, my Little Negra.

Capoeira Dancers. Ceramic tile. Artist unknown. Bahia, Brazil, 1968.

Macumba Dancers by Chico Sampaio. Woodcut. 1968. Salvador, Bahia, Brazil

Macumba Dancer at Candomblé celebration. Barbara Young. 1997.

Trobador with Berimbou by Chico Sampaio 1968 Salvador

Oxací. Wood Sculpture. Artist unknown. 1968

64. The Serpent

Adams County, Ohio 1846

THE UNIQUE EARTHEN MOUND had presence, something the farmer felt but could not describe. Instead of disturbing the mound to cultivate and plant corn, the farmer contacted the Historical Society. Word of the find spread. Surveyors from the East Coast traveled to Ohio to see. The men sketched the mound and give the sculpture a name, "The Serpent." They petitioned the State of Ohio to preserve the earthen sculpture as a historical site.

1946.

I AM FOUR. Mother took me on an outing to visit The Serpent. She drove the '42 blue Chevy, along Rt. 73, a two-lane county road in southern Ohio, just miles north of the Ohio River. The cornfields, planted up to the edge of the road, were laden with ears ready to be picked, taken home for dinner, and smeared with butter. Add sliced fresh red sun-kissed tomatoes and you have a tasty summer supper. We pass a yellow-and-black caution traffic sign picturing a horse and buggy. Mother said this was the way Amish farmers did their visiting and church going. I hoped to see an Amish farmer, but today we were the only ones on the road. Somewhere, around the next curve, we would find a break in the endless rows of corn for the entrance into the state park.

We entered a slight incline into a wooded park of deciduous trees harboring beautiful conical grassy mounds, perfectly shaped as if rolled by hand just as my grandmother made her round biscuits on the wood stove. Mom pulls the car into a parking spot near the wooden structure pit toilet.

It smells awful. I carefully lift the wooden hole cover and wiggle my bottom onto the seat without looking into the depths. I know what is there and do not want to slip and drop anything below. Pumped from a deep well, the water to wash hands is icy cold.

In sharp contrast, the freshness and the green of the park is fragrant, and the trees rustle a soft welcome. Mom and I stop briefly at the cabin reception station to register, pay our parking fee, and glance at the small gift shop of post cards and mementos. A narrow concrete path leads to a tall metal lookout tower. I follow mom up two flights and look out to the trees, almost shaking hands with the top branches which congratulate me for climbing so high. Leaning against the railing, I look down on a large earthen serpent as if sculptured by giants, a land snake that wiggles itself across the top of the cliff and looks out to a crevice in the valley, a breach in the surrounding hills. Near the cliff, the mouth of the snake is about to swallow an egg.

The breeze at this tower height ruffles my hair, lifts the skirt of my dress, and speaks to me of something ancient, as if wisdom is being wafted through the wind. This serpent mound was built for a purpose, and it is not a children's play area. I listen to the song of birds as if they would share the secrets of who came before us to build it, but the birds were content to be about their daily business, soothing, chatting, nesting, mothers looking after their young as my mother did for me.

I carefully descend the tower, listening to the tinny vibration, the click of my heels on metal steps. Safely down, I feel grounded and not so exposed at the heights. The narrow path continues to the sculpture, mimicking its undulations across the field. Walking beside the large earthen snake, I sense being protected by its prominence. Beyond the mound at the edge of the cliff, I look out across the valley and hear water gurgling in Brush Creek, flowing below the cliff. The rustle of the trees whispers of family. I am happy here, like being in Ruth Ross's Sunday School class surrounded by those who love me. It is a feeling of spirit, like being in the chapel with light shining through the Tiffany stained-glass window. Here, warm sunrays streak through the tree branches and rest upon the snake mound. I feel a reverence in this serpent mound and am at peace.

Chic'hen Itza, Mexico 2010

I AM SIXTY-EIGHT. Clearing customs at Cancun on the Yucatan Peninsula, Mexico, I board a bus for Chic 'hen Itza to visit the ancient ruins of a Mayan civilization, long gone from the area. I stand in front of El Castillo to study the steps, by count 91 to the top of the Temple. Times four sides of the temple equal 364 steps. The top central step adds one more which total 365. The Mayans were mathematicians and astrologers who built an observatory to study the movement of the sun, stars, and planets. They knew when to plant and when to celebrate the harvest.

Thousands gather at the summer solstice to witness the sun's shadow upon the steps of the Temple at Chic 'hen Itza. At this precise time of light and shadow, phenomena happen. A snake slithers down the steps in plain view of those who have come to celebrate. Although I am not present for the solstice celebration of this event, I image the serpent moving down the steps of the Temple, just as they said it would.

2015

I AM SEVENTY-THREE. When I return to Ohio for a 55th high school reunion, I make a pilgrimage, and drive the road in Adams County to visit

The Serpent. The metal tower is still there, and still tinny sounding when my heels tread the metal steps. I climb the two flights, and again a bit winded when I reach the deck. The trees, children of those before them, reside beside the tower and communicate their permanence. The concrete walk is the same with grass growing in the cracks. The serpent is the same—magnificent, mysterious still, and not as tall as I remember. The serpent silently awaits the return of the solstice to appear in the valley of Brush Creek. The gift shop is displaying on bookshelves titles of the Mound Builders of the Mississippi Valley and several books of the Mayans and their calendars. I purchase three, reading the same authors of the books I saw when I shopped in the gift stores at Chic 'hen Itza. Are there not connections of my Ohio serpent to the serpent which slithered down the steps of the Temple at Chic 'hen Itza? Might the Mayan civilization that disappeared from the Yucatan, have migrated across the Gulf to Florida, and north into the heartland of America? I speculate this connection and know that other authors are researching the movement.

"Will you be coming back to celebrate the solstice with us? The receptionist asks.

"Yes," I reply.

Adams County, Ohio 2021

I AM SEVENTY-NINE, and Serpent Mound continues to call me back. On a road trip from Cincinnati to Hanover, Pennsylvania to visit my brother, I travel Rt. 73, stop, and pay my respects to The Serpent. My trip continued to the Ohio River, through the mountains of West Virginia, to historic Cumberland, Maryland, and on to Gettysburg and Hanover.

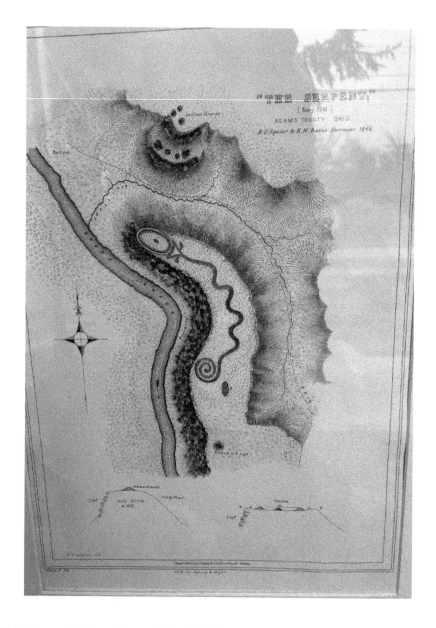

"The Serpent," Adams County, Ohio. E.G. Squier & E.H. Davis, Surveyor 1846. Believed to be the work of Mound Builders, the Adena and Hopewell Peoples.

65. Diversity Panel

Ceramics studio 2011

TURQUOISE, COBALT CARBONATE, CHROME OXIDE—a smidgen of one or more of each material I place together on the weigh scale. I pour the mixture into a small plastic container with a tight-fitting lid. Celadon and 2% iron oxide is the next mixture onto the weigh scale. This combination is poured out of the mixing bowl into another container. The third mixture is deep red copper and golden copper 1%. Under heat, these powders become glazes. Ceramic pieces onto which these glazes will be applied, emerge after firing in the kiln as vivid colors, unlike their powered dullness and texture. They become black, mottled green, strong blue, purple, light green, medium brown.

I am following *mais of minus* (more or less) the formulas of mixing glazes in the ceramic lab at the community college. The fan in the mixing lab is on so I do not inhale toxic fumes that emerge from the combinations. The alchemy of the powders will perform magic. I wait until the end of the process to see how these earthen elements have interacted. I set the glaze mixtures aside to build the clay facial figures to which I will apply these glazes.

I lift a block of white clay to the canvas covered worktable. I, like the clay to be molded, am shaped by my interventions with elements of the earth and contact with the soil of my birth. With a thin wire, I slice a hunk of clay from the block and throw it onto the table, punching it, getting to know its pliability. The clay's unique mixture of wet, elastic earthen soil particles relinquishes itself to the kneading of my hands, like a loaf of bread stretching with manipulation. I massage the clay, connecting with its heritage and possession of knowledge, with the materials with which it has resided in the earth for millions of years. The clay body surrenders itself to what it is to become. Personalities emerge as my fingers play with facial features, and I move these pieces to the waiting-in-line shelf for their first bisque firing in the kiln, from which they will exit ready for glazing. After glazing the bisque forms, the pieces return to the kiln for a second firing.

Consider our human mixture of heritages. Each creation is unique. Like the ceramic glazes, human unions produce people of various shades of skin color, beautifully blended. Beneath the human creation, personalities, talents, resolve, persistence, and survival merge. As a young Presbyterian fourth grader memorizing bible passages for confirmation, I remember the passage on talents. Something like, "Do not hide your talents under a basket." I consider each human blending, a unique creation, full of talents to be shared.

Retrieving the first fired bisque forms, I apply my mixtures of glazes, mating one glaze with another. These ceramic pieces return to the shelf to wait their second firing. When my small portraitures emerge and are placed together for review before the professor, I call them collectively, "*Diversity Panel.*" The professor smiles, nods in agreement.

"Diversity Panel." In ceramic lab I created test tiles to explore variances in glazes

66. Prayers

2014

LOOKING AT THE MONITOR, I saw an X-ray of the skull and spine with a grey spot, the offending tumor. I saw the history of Emily's life flash before me—birth in Cincinnati, moving on her first birthday to Virginia, growing up among the azaleas, rhododendron, and dogwoods, moving west to enter kindergarten in Texas and learning to ride and own a horse. When I divorced her father, the two of us moved again, and she entered junior high school in Washington state. The neurosurgeon was explaining his procedure, speaking to me, the terrified mother: "You can see on the monitor the tumor is at the base of the skull. We will use a laser beam with pinpoint accuracy to cauterize the tumor. My surgical team will make a helmet for Emily which will secure her head to the surgical table. She will be unable to move her head."

Surgery of the brain and spinal column frightened me, and I had to trust in the competence of the neurosurgeon and new technology that made this surgical procedure possible. Emily's brain power was not shabby. For two years, her academic decathlon high school team represented Washington state in national competition. Emily won Honorable Mention in the national competition in mathematics. After taking all the science courses offered at the community college, she went on to graduate from Washington State University with a bachelor's degree in Genetics and Cell Biology. I was proud of her accomplishments and respectful of her abilities.

A piece of mesh plastic sheet was heated and molded to Emily's face with a connecting sheet wrapped around the back of her head. The mask molded to her unique features and contour and screwed into place, making her immobile for the laser trajectory, a procedure called Trilogy. This procedure was quite different from the ancient brain surgery, inserting a stylus into the brain to allow evil spirits to exit. After surgery, Emily gave me the two pieces of the plastic head shield, serving as a model I could study in the ceramic studio. I would make six healing masks, prayers kneaded into the clay to form a shield against illness, prayers offered for Emily's complete recovery.

Trilogy Mesh Shield

Healing Prayer Mask 1. Clay, raku fired

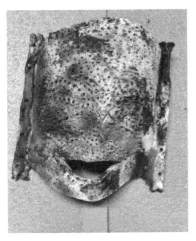

Healing Prayer Mask 2. Clay

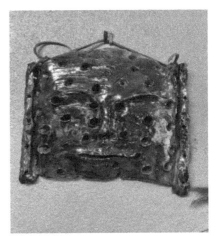

Healing Prayer Mask 3. Clay, Cedar, Leather

Healing Prayer Mask 4. Raku fired

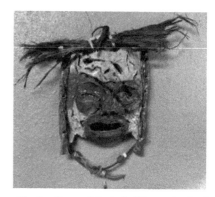

Healing Prayer Mask 5. Clay, raku fired.

67. Tree Spirit

WALKING ON A FOREST TRAIL, a strip of tree bark fell near the path. I picked up the piece, felt the striations of texture, and marveled at the subtle coloring. At first, this piece of bark looked weathered gray. Holding it in my hands, I discovered other colors—smudges of black among brown, pink, and ivory. The gray became a muted palette, the texture softer. I wondered if the tree had shed this bark as a piece of outgrown clothing.

On another walk, I noticed four-inch, black-with-white-spots bird feathers, the spots a polka dot pattern. I knelt to gather them, caressing the silky feel, and stroking the fibers together. I thought of John Hancock pictured signing the Declaration of Independence with a quill, the feather of a larger bird. The small feathers I held in my hand were not quill quality, but ones to be appreciated for their simple beauty and for their task protecting the bird which shed them.

I pick up these bits of nature here and there because they speak to me - smooth and warm beach stones tossed by the sea, leaves of various shapes – pointed oak, big maple to be a model for a slab of clay, needles of pine to be woven into baskets. Nature pieces, like the bark and the tiny feathers, might end up in an art piece or treasured as they are.

In the studio, I paint my mask the colors of the bark strip. The polka dot feathers I attach to the bark. I dump on the table buttons from my mother's tall mason jar, two buttons from an old work shirt. Colors of the bark, are selected. At the time, I had no back story for which I could explain this art piece. Or that is what I thought

Friend Seth, a former council member of the Cowlitz Indian Tribe stood quietly studying the finished mask hanging on the wall in my home. "You have made an image of Wakan Tanka. It is the Tree Spirit. The Great Mystery."

When I visit the Grove of the Patriarchs near Packwood, or walk into the neighborhood of friend Robin's treehouse, hike to the summit of Mt. Elinor in the Olympics, spend the night in the volunteer campground near Longmire, or lose myself on the trails of Mt. Rainier, I am transported into a different space. A calming presence, away from the constant hum of the freeway, sheltered from lists of tasks, calls, and people and their facial coverings. I am given the freedom to be present with myself and with the natural environment. I melt into the naturalness and listen. I wonder why I had not taken the time before to listen, see, walk among these trees with so many years of collected wisdom. I will tell you a story.

1996

FROM THE RESERVATION, I received a summons to appear at court in Houston, over child support with the husband I had left in Texas. I was now working on an isolated reservation just north of the confluence of the Columbia River and Pacific Ocean, far distance for the court room in Texas. Late in the afternoon, two Native teachers from Bay Center visited the tribal community center. I listened to their story of ancestors of the Lower Chehalis Peoples who fled to an island to escape the ravages of smallpox, measles and flu, diseases brought by the white settlers and decimating tribal families. The Ancestors described themselves as the Canoe People and paddled to the island in the bay, and there took respite from illness. The island remains uninhabited today, and the only access is by water.

"You do not have to make the trip to Houston," my co-worker Joan explained. "Instead, reduce your stress. Do something special for yourself. Let the court system in Texas speak for you." Hearing the visitors' story of the old growth trees which had been on the island since before anyone knew, I needed and wanted to go to the island in the bay. I sought calming and respite.

It was five o'clock and the office was closing for this Thursday evening. Forgetting about a report due in Washington, D.C. on Friday, I could think only of Joan's words "Reduce stress. Do something special for yourself." I filled out a mental health leave for the next day, failing to give my whereabouts. I reached for the phone and called a friend—a tall, handsome, bearded Scotsman, Captain John, who had once been a tugboat captain in the Port of Tacoma and now ran a boat taxi service, moored in Nachatta, an oyster capital of the North Pacific coast. I wanted the captain to be available to ferry me to the isolated island. I called home to tell my daughter, a senior in high school, my sudden plans, where I would be, and that I would return home to Olympia Saturday.

As the lights at the tribal community center were turned low, I headed the Honda in the direction of Nachatta on the far side of the inlet bay. The two-lane road hugged the side of the bay, and I noted the invasive spartina grasses extending their reach into the water. These were a bane to the environmental team at the reservation. Ghost shrimp, too, had invaded the local oyster beds. Both the spartina and the ghost shrimp were concerns of the tribe as they built their oyster business. My drive continued through the town of South Bend, hugging the curves at the eastern end of the bay.

I smiled as I drove thinking of the good-looking captain waiting dinner for me. The road was like a snake wiggling between the bay and a cliff. I maneuvered each curve slowly to avoid meeting a driver from the opposite direction. But few were on the road at this time of evening. I see the sign announcing the entrance to a wildlife preserve; then, the sign that directed people to higher ground in case of tsunami and looked for the path those in danger would take should such an event happen. So isolated was this road for a sudden exit from danger, I shuddered to think of it. An eagle flew overhead, a good sign. A doe and her fawn darted across the road and quickly disappeared into the trees. Across a narrow wood bridge and on around the next curve, I began to relax, feeling a kinship with the animals and waters. The drive was pleasant, quiet, giving me time to consider what I was doing and why, so spontaneous were my actions, devoid of forward planning.

In about two hours, I reached the captain's home located across the road from the dock where his launch was tethered, waiting. The house was an old Victorian built in the days of prime oyster fishing. It was beautifully landscaped with colorful flowers due to John's attentive gardening. A large garage contained all sorts of boating equipment – ropes, cranks, pulleys, small craft, kayak, canoe, and rowboat. A chicken coop was out back, so his egg supply was current. A hand paved stone walk connected the drive to the back door. I knocked to announce my presence. John answered with a wide grin.

"Good to see you. Come in. How was the drive? Before you answer, supper is ready. We're having oyster stew, fresh homemade bread, greens from the garden and paired with chilled chardonnay."

"So good to see you again. The drive was pleasant with few on the road. Saw an eagle. And your dinner sounds wonderful! I'm hungry."

John's peppered beard had grown another inch since I had last seen him. His moustache was starting to cover his upper lip. His hazel eyes twinkled with fun, and although he usually smelled of the salty sea and of boat motors, I could also smell the kitchen in full preparation for a tasty dinner. The table was set with a view of the harbor.

"Ring……. ring…." John answered his phone. It was my daughter. "Mom, your boss called and asked about the report due in Washington tomorrow."

"Thanks, I will take care of it. So glad you called and let me know." I called my boss.

"Mr. Chairman, I am so sorry. I got so wound up in the story of the island, common business sense left me."

"Barbara, I wish you would have told me your plans. I could have been better prepared when Washington called. Request an extension. Be sure that you have received confirmation your request was received tomorrow, the due date for the report."

"Yes, I will do that Mr. Chairman. Thank you for understanding." I hung up the phone feeling depressed. I had skipped out on my responsibility forgetting about the report being due the next day. Worse, I had put my boss in an awkward position with the grant office in D.C. Phooey! Now, I had to think of how, in this isolated place I would deliver my report.

"I have a FAX machine," John proposed, "and you have paper and pen. Write your request for extension, and we can send it from here. In the morning, we will ask for confirmation of receipt." With a plan in place, I could smile, and turn my attention to a lovely dinner by the bay.

John's home was warm and pleasant, filled with art pictures of nautical scenes, fitting well into the background bay. Across the street near to the dock were mounds of oyster shells. As we ate, we planned the next day's trip on accessing the isolated island. After dinner, we gathered gear, jackets, food, water and studied the tide tables. We retired early to get an early start the next day.

Confirming the FAX was received and dated in Washington, D.C., we prepared for departure to the island. It was high tide, and the sun was rising over the bay. As seven cormorants watched from the top of pilings and one bald eagle from a solo sentinel, the captain turned the boat smoothly, despite the bay's choppy waters and strong gathering wind. Gripping the port railing, and facing into the wind, I let my hair blow and relaxed with the soothing hum of the engine. Gazing out to the open water, I was feeling okay I had spoken for this outing.

About an hour and a half later, we glided into a cove of the island. John steered the boat to about three feet of depth, cut the engine, and dropped anchor. We rolled up our jeans above knees, removed shoes and socks and climbed over the gunnel into the icy water. The quarter-sized pebbles under my feet were smooth, round, and shifted gently as I waded to shore. The captain carried a long heavy rope and wound it around a study cedar at the forest edge, tethering the boat securely. We sat on the sand to re-sock and shoe. Slinging backpacks in place, we entered the forest.

As I absorbed the quiet beauty of the island, I felt no need to speak. I was present in a sanctuary with old growth cedar, sunlight streaking through the branches, filling me with wonder, peace, and love. It was not unlike the feeling I had standing in the sanctuary of the Presbyterian Church, sunlight streaking through the colors of the stained-glass window, sending rainbows across the pews. Within the silence of this place, one felt the wisdom of time, the support of strength, the presence of spirit.

Departing the narrow path, I walked to a giant tree, and placed my open palms upon its bark, feeling the ridges and bumps of its time and growth in the forest. Like an old woman with deep wrinkles in her face, the tree had deep ruts that spoke of wisdom earned. Awed at this tree's girth, I circumnavigated its trunk, climbed over its roots firmly implanted in the ground, marveling its interconnectedness with younger trees, communicating through roots systems. This tree could be the ancestor storyteller speaking of history, informing the young of their heritage, the journey and protocol for all those within the forest. With my palms on the tree, I gave it my blessing. Holding that position, I allowed the spirit of the tree to flow into my hands.

Walking on through the forest, I opened myself to the spirit of these ancestors. Palpable in an environment of strength, I felt my stress lifting. The anxiety of my divorce was replaced with a sense of calm knowing. A few large tree trunks had weathered footholds, evidence early lumbermen had once been here to selectively log. Yet even these trunks recovered from the insult, allowing seedlings to nourish within their bark, offering themselves to foster forest growth. They were nursing next generations.

The tides were moving out. John untethered the boat. We rolled up pant legs, removed shoes and socks and returned to the boat in time not to be beached on the island for the night. Any longer and waters would rush out from under the anchor. As the boat calmly and slowly reversed its direction for home port, both the Captain and I were quiet, relaxing with the warmth of the day, the success of the excursion, and thought of the evening to come.

All in the space of one day, the tenue of the trees, the silence of the forest, and the moving waters calmed me. After a dinner of fried oysters, various greens freshly tossed, and bottle of wine, we debriefed.

Thus ends my story of how Tree Spirit Mask came to be.

I picked up a piece of bark. Found small feathers laying in my path. Carried them home. Painted a plaster of Paris facial form in the colors of the bark. I connected with the tree spirit.

68. Eagles' Nest: Behind the Welding Mask

2015

WHEN I TOLD WELDING PROFESSOR JOHN GROSS THAT I AM AFRAID of fire and gas in welding, he invites me to sign up for class and learn how to weld. Saturday mornings, the welding shop is occupied by devoted community students who fabricate art projects and help each other practice the skills of arc and meg welding. For resources, we pay a small fee to rummage the dumpster for used and discarded metal materials.

Mary has long legs, and she is able to hook her feet into the steel steps and swing her leg over the rim of the trash bin searching scrap metal. I could stretch my legs to the first steps and poke my head over the rim, but I am not so agile to climb into the inside of the dumpster. At eye level just over the rim, I perused the screens, pipes, twisted rods, rusty whatever's and steel practice pieces of serious welding students. Surely there was something of value that could be recycled into a grand and glorious steel sculpture that could be displayed on the Percival Landing Plinths. I so wanted to be an exhibit artist. Alexander Calder was my visual mentor. I have not the strength for Caldwell size of construction, but I could find something in the bin to perk my creativity.

I saw a steel mesh screen I wanted. Mary said she would get it for me, and she fashioned a long stick-like probe to dig it out. She wedged the probing rod under the mesh and lifted it up and over to where my arm was reaching over the bin rim to retrieve it. We connected and I tossed the treasure over the rim to land with a thud onto the asphalt parking lot. My eyes spotted a triangular piece welded to a solid flat foot-long, quarter-inch

253

piece of steel. I had to have that piece and would decide later just what it was or how it could be used.

"Mary, I want the pointed triangle on the steel base, please, the piece buried among the steel bits and pieces. "Yes, that one right there; It's a beauty!"

"Well, what's it for?" Mary asks.

"I have no idea, but I want it."

"For you, I will get it." Mary lifts heftier pieces out of the way to reach it. It is very heavy, but she can get it to the edge of the dumpster. The piece was like an Egyptian pyramid, had the same structural integrity and was welded to a nice steel base. I carry this treasure into the grinding room along with my circular grinder. Put it on the table and secure the pyramid with a vise; put on my clear plastic face shield, insert ear plugs, and plug the cord into the wall socket. I push the button. Grinding wheel spins into action. Rust is challenged; sparks fly like a July 4th sparkler. A shiny polished piece of steel emerges. Brush strokes of the grinding wheel became whisked into the smooth flat steel sides of the pyramid.

I sat with my mesh screens that Mary retrieved from the bin and visualized how they might be transformed into various wavy, interesting shapes. I walked to the corner of the shop where I could use the plasma cutter that uses a directed torch to "cut," or melt, the thick steel. At the wall, I turned the air tube to open, and connected the heavy rounded amp plug with the curved prongs into its specific wall socket. On the end of the plasma cutter, I attached three fitted tips together to make the needed electrical connections. The clamp grounder was attached to the steel table where I would be working. I donned my welding helmet and placed my hands into padded protective gloves. The tabletop was an open grate with a collecting bin. I was wearing proper leather boots and clothes of 100% natural fibers, as no synthetic clothing was allowed in shop. I reviewed that the plasma cutter was connected properly. When I held the torch within 1/16th to 1/8th of the steel mesh, the focused flame melted the steel. With no pattern in mind and holding tightly to the torch, I moved up, around, and back and forth like a snake slithering through high grass leaving an interesting trail and succeeded in my goal of reducing the mesh screen to small unique, interesting, shaped pieces.

Returning to my stockpile of steel odds and ends, thrown out student practice pieces and other pieces of discarded metal projects, I looked over the supply to see what I could cut into diverse shapes. In nature, little found is uniform. My selection of mesh and steel pieces went next to the giant roller for curvature. Taking hours to gently roll back and forth, I became mesmerized by the movement watching closely that my fingers did not get caught between the rollers. The curved pieces of steel piled up on each other and began to take their own shape on their own volition.

"Hey, that looks like a bird's nest" Mary said as she passed my work bench on her way to the forge.

"Yes, it does," I responded and wondered if my steel pieces were in some way organically re-arranging themselves, congregating in community. There must be attraction one for the other, gravitating into a unified whole. Or, I could be hallucinating with the mystery of the fire, rollers, grinding that takes place behind dark masks. It was time for a break.

After breathing in the fresh air of summer, I collected helmet, wire cutters, magnets to hold pieces in place, gloves, welding tip, cone, spacer, and connector, and headed to a cubby space for MIG welding. The acetylene and oxygen tanks were turned on. I tested the oxygen for an appropriate pressure and turned on the cubby light and fan. I checked to see that the "on" button was pressed within my welding helmet. I turned on the appropriate wire speed to about 17.4 and secured the grounding clamp to the steel table. If everything was in place and connected, I was ready to weld.

I let one piece of steel ease into a companion piece of steel and secured the two pieces together with a magnet. The pieces did that, select where they wanted to be within this collection of pieces. If the placement was not right, the piece was repelled and fell away. If it was right, it fit and stayed snugly in its placement. I pushed the button of the welding tool and caused the mesh wires to melt the tiny cross pieces in place. Starting with a stronger base, the various shapes began to come together.

Eagles will fly miles to find the correct shaped pieces to build the nest. I journeyed to the trash bin, the shopping cart of discarded material, and to my own garage collection of steel treasurers. I collected thrown-away wire in the gutter outside the fence of a construction site in Louisville when I was in the city for a national competitive swim. I picked up a well smooshed steel can that a garbage truck left behind on an immaculately clean street in Houston. Human and eagles search, find, and build their nests.

I remembered the triangular piece of steel that Mary had dug out of the trash bin and which I had so carefully shined by grinding away the rust. I took the pyramid shape to the nest to see if they were compatible. The nest fit comfortably on the pyramid and settled down upon the tip to secure its nesting position off the surface of the ground or table or wherever the nest was to be laid. The triangular pyramid shape became the base on which the nest perched.

In the show room of the Monarch Sculpture Park Gallery, "Eagle's Nest" became ensconced upon a pedestal among impressive sculptures of wood and stone. Large paintings hung on the walls. Comfortable in its placement, I left the show room. On the way home, I stopped by a senior swimming buddy, Evelyn's house, to tell her of the art exhibit. She said that she would have her daughter drive her to the show when it opened two days hence.

Evelyn was good to her word. On the arm of her daughter, she visited every piece in the show, savoring the artistic creativity of each artist. She had been an art teacher in the Tenino school system and had inspired many a young artist. After visiting the entire collection, Evelyn came to me with a check, purchasing Eagles' Nest. The metal sculpture was later placed in the foyer of the entrance to her home, a home snug among the trees and overlooking a lake, a perfect place for an eagles' nest.

Time passes. Three months from the time we hugged goodbye, I was informed at swim workout of Evelyn's passing. She had slipped into her next journey. Relatives and friends celebrated her life, all ninety-seven plus years of it at a grand gala dance at the senior center where each Wednesday from 2:00 to 4:00, on the arm of her elegant dance partner, Evelyn, in a beautiful ballroom gown had always been the star performer. Her vitality and positive approach to life, her encouragement to fellow swimmers, which included my granddaughter and me when we swam in her lake, her gold metal swim at Stanford a few years before, and her own art which hangs on the wall behind *Eagles' Nest* are all testaments of Evelyn's love of life. I think *Eagles' Nest* gave her pleasure and inspiration to take her next flight.

69. Skipping Through the Gallery

AMONG THE FIRST PEOPLES of the coastal Pacific Northwest, there is a legend of the Wild Woman of the Woods, *Dzunukwa*. She carries a basket on her back, and collects children who have been bad, misbehaved, or did not listen to their elders. *Dzunukwa* stalks the community and catches the children, puts them into her basket, and takes them home to eat.

It is a lesson for all children to obey, and not

Dzunuwka (Dza-noo-qua). Ceramic, cedar strips, walnut shell earrings

to wander into the deep forest.

N'kisi N'kondi is the figure of agreement, of reconciliation, of mediation, of dispute resolution, a common figure frequently made of wood, and found in the Congo. A feuding couple may come before *N'kisi* and present their case. When an agreement is made, the resolution is nailed into the wooden figure or otherwise attached to *N'kisi*, a binding arbitration.

N'kisi N'kondi. Steel sculpture. 2010. Olympia

258

Open hands welcome those coming for consultation to resolve conflict. "Agreements" here are etched into metal pieces and screwed into the sculpture's body. In the original wood carved figures of *N'kisi N'kondi*, agreements were nailed to the figure.

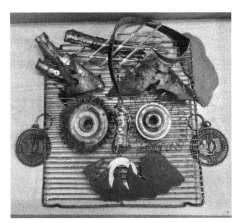

Waiting for Weld. Mixed media

Listening and observing, these steel pieces wait for the weld. What fun I've had with classmates as we scoured and dug through the discarded practice pieces of welding students or found interesting scraps in the recycle bin. We foraged the dumpster, reexamined the trash, looked for the treasure no one else wanted. Each piece we uncovered carried a charm all its own and exhibited a personality, talent, gleam, or shape, and when added to the other pieces, created a more magnificent whole.

Enlightenment overcomes Darkness.

Education defeats ignorance.

As the sun rises to shine,

Night slips away.

"Enlightenment." Clay and wire.

The art and story of hair is personal. In the 1960's my first husband Ken and I were part of the Hippie Generation, and we let our hair grow long and un-styled. Ken preferred to draw his straight brown hair tinged with red into a ponytail which style he retained for the rest of his life. Even when his hair became increasingly thin, gray, and bald on top, his ponytail remained in place. In high school days, I used to put large foam pink rollers into my hair at night so I could awake in the morning transforming my thin straight hair into wavy curls. Once, in college, I tried to curl my straight hair and let my roommate give me a perm, turning my

Hair. Steel

head into a tightly curled auburn dust mop. Now in my late seventies with thinning, short hair, I get my trim at the barber shop. We are fussing with hair.

Hair is control and political statement. Indian children taken from their home reservations and put into religious schools far from tribal traditions were sheared of their braids and forced to conform to a severe dominant culture hair style. In current times, hair style of any race can no longer be legally discriminatory for job opportunities and advancement, school attendance, or in any way, ostracized.

On April 29, 1968, the musical *Hair* opened on Broadway depicting the counterculture and sexual revolution of the late sixties. Several songs became anthems of the Vietnam War era peace movement. Although there was initial resistance to the initiation of what is a "rock musical," the production of Hair ran for over 1700 performances and moved on to London for over 1900 more. The musical, bursting out of traditional theater, expressed youthful energy, boldly confronted political issues, and protested the need for war. Hair styles became political statements of self-identity.

Dad Phillip with corded hair; Puppy son Zander, uncut, natural

My daughter's breed stud, Phillip, a black standard poodle service dog and his puppy son Zander show off their hair styles. Phillip's hair is twisted into cords, an official style defined by the AKC (American Kennel Club) while the four-month-old son Zander shows off his uncut fluffy puppy hair. Zander's thick hair belies his trim build.

70. Clay Voice: The Soul of Soil

Millions of years ago, I was in process of creation
Existing before humans, before animals, before time itself
Soaking, absorbing, hugging particles resting upon my soul
Feeling the heat of volcanoes
Harboring silica dropping into my lap
Riding the rumble of earth shaking beneath me
Moving as I must with the overlapping of plates
Cradling tiny creatures who burrow my grains
Each adding life and spirit to my quiet waiting

I see the sun rising in the east, warming me,
bringing me light and a new day
I vision red-orange sunsets
Bringing peace and the coolness of night
Tiny creatures cuddle close feeling heat
I've retained from sun's warmth
We partner in building inclusiveness

One day humans came to find me
sifting through their fingers my collected wisdom
of years waiting, absorbing, experiencing
climate changes, animals coming and going,
water seeping in and moving on
"This clay is perfect," they exclaim!
Thrilled for my textured existence

I am cut and shaped into blocks
Transported to a ceramic art studio
Students slice away a chunk
Fondling it with their hands

Rolling, slapping, flattening, shaping
I move, change to become their image
They were calmed, pleased with my presence.

With her fingers, a ceramic student
massages slurp into my crown
Together with classmates, carries me to Ocean Shores
Digging into the sand, a cozy kiln.
Among the wood, sawdust, paper products,
I snuggle deeper into the warm beach
feel again one with the earth

A fire is lit
Bake us through the night
Listening to the coming and going of tides,
I submit to the fires of the kiln
Nestling into the warmth of flames
Emerging the next morning with a contented smile
loving the creation, I came to be

Clay Voice: Soul of Soil

71. Mandarin Chinese in Translation

Beijing, China 1999

IN THE INTRODUCTION TO PART IV, the poem noted the women of the tribe gave me permission to take the healing power of mask making into the world. Chapter 56 discusses mask making at the scientific conference. Chapter 68 describes a workshop I facilitated for the Nurse Training School, University of Beijing. Building art story masks crosses cultural barriers to understanding. Mask Making brings a diverse world into partnership.

Instead of taking the underground subway, my sponsors at Beijing University insisted upon a chauffeured car pick-up. Weaving in and out of street traffic among peddle carts, thousands of bicycles, and small slow transports, I arrived at the university to face a room of eager nursing students sitting at their desks. Each desk was precisely placed in six straight rows. Anxious to begin with the visiting American nurse professor, they silently faced the front podium, and waited for introductions.

I felt rattled from the hustled approach to campus, but the faces of the students filled with anticipation inspired me. The simultaneous translator backed me up. I was not used to students in rows and attentively hearing every word I uttered. I explained that I needed to work with students in a circle. Confused at first with such instructions, I made a circle with my arms. The translator did her best to explain. The students rose to move their desks into an unprecedented formation, and an oblong shape emerged. I explained that a circle allowed each to see the other. They rose again and moved their chairs into a nicely shaped circle. I was satisfied and they were pleased to have accomplished the task. I spoke in English; the translator interpreted into Mandarin. When the students responded in Chinese, the translator interpreted to me in English. We planned our day together and soon left the circle to go to worktables.

Utilizing oblong tables positioned against tall windows shedding light on the work, students set up to make masks using plaster of Paris gauze strips. Soft tonal chatter accompanied construction and it seemed not long before the class was painting and decorating their creations. Later, we reconvened in the circle, held up the decorated masks and each student told the story that accompanied the mask. The translator was speaking rapidly not to miss a word of the presentations as well as the English translation. The beauty of the storytelling was that I was sensing similar stories that came from workshops conducted in my own town in America. Leaning over to my dedicated translator, I told her. "Please listen to these stories without concern for my translation. Even though I do not speak your language, I understand what the storyteller is saying because the translation is in the art, and the story is from the heart."

The translator and I listened to the beauty of expression and the stories in the mask presentations. When all within the circle had spoken, it was time to end class. Even though we had been together the entire day, it was time to leave. The circle was replaced with neat rows, desks one behind the other, neatly in order. I could have taken my tape measure to check accuracy of placement. Carrying their story masks, relaxed, and smiling, the students departed.

With everything in its proper place with no evidence of the day's events, the headmaster and nurse instructors brought out drinks, treats, snacks, and all sorts of tasty savories. We toasted to a most successful cross-cultural adventure.

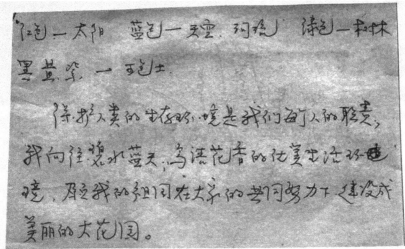

Red -- presents the sun. Blue -- the sky. Green -- trees.
Black, yellow and purple -- the earth.

It is everyone's duty to protect the ecological environment of human race. I yearn for a beautiful living surrounding where birds sing and flowers give forth fragrance. I hope my homeland will be built into a beautiful big garden with the common effort made by all the people in our country.

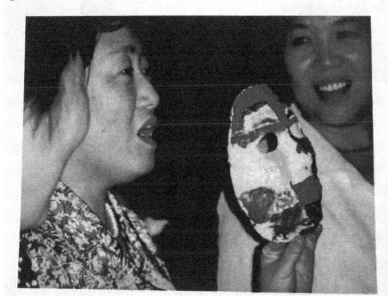

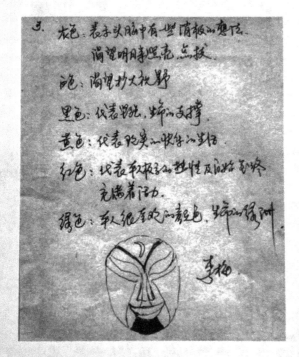

Gray: There are negative thoughts in my mind, and I
      look forward to bright moon that shine on me.
White: Looking forward to broaden my horizon
Black: Strong will, support of life
Yellow: Happy life in reality
Red: I am always very enthusiastic and full of vigor and
      energy all my life
Green: My favorite color – the oasis of life
                  Li, Mei

我有一个幸福，美好的家庭

我的女儿是我心中的明月，为我带来希望和未来。
太阳代表我的丈夫，他是我们家庭中的支柱
是我们家庭的骄傲。星星代表我自己。我们三
人缺一不可。在我们的生活中虽然有风，雨，雷，电
但是我们一家人生活一起，就像一座屹然不动的山
经得起大风大浪

I have a nice, happy family. My daughter is the bright moon in my mind who brings me hope and future. The sun stands for my husband. He is the supportive pillar of the family. We feel proud of him. Stars are myself. We three are a unity, depending upon one another and unable to separate. There are high winds, thunderstorms, but we can stand tall and strong with three of us being together just like a mountain.

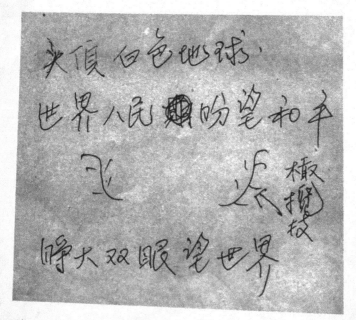

There stands a white earth on the top (crown) of the head.
The people all over the world yearn for peace.

Olive branch – a symbol of peace

Open the eyes wide to see the world.

270

Whether in Beijing, Washington, D.C., Philadelphia, Chicago, or Olympia, the circles were similar in the mask storytelling. Stories of family, children, loss, love, hope, and peace. Stories of life lived. I am pleased that the women of the circle taught me to make masks and to share that skill to whomever is willing to sit, meditate, allow someone to touch them, and to have the opportunity of touching another. It is in the telling of our stories, that we can love ourselves and come to understand our place in the universe.

V. Epilogue

2020-2021

SHELTERED IN PLACE, retired from a daily job, having a comfortable home and food to eat, I have time to reflect. I am revealing to you how my not asking the tough questions caused my daughters to suffer with hidden domestic violence. Hear my voice through my letters to you, Dear Readers.

72. Letters

Sheltered-in-place at home

Olympia, Washington

September 1, 2020

Dear Reader,

It has been fifty-five years, since my first marriage to Ken and our work with Peace Corps in Brazil. Forty-five years, since I met Freddie McMurray in the divorced and singles group of the Methodist Church. Thirty years, since I backed out of a Texas driveway and drove across the country to Washington state.

I was blinded when I married second husband. If I applied the eye-chart exam to attain a 2020 vision, in hindsight this is what it would read:

I

W A S

S E T U P

I picked up the pen to write, because I wanted to know why I was unable to raise questions or to speak more strongly. Being the third-born in my family, I wonder if I let others do the speaking, and I, the listening.

Visiting on Parents Weekend in Emily's freshman year at Washington State University, we did not go to the football game, but instead, to the rat lab where Emily was installing tiny cannulas into rats' brains, assisting the professor studying the effects of alcohol on the brain. Emily also showed me the rehabilitative raptor cage where an eagle with a broken wing was recovering. She was given a license to collect roadkill for the forensic lab.

During our tour of the Science Building, we studied a wall chart of Nobel Prize winners.

"You know, Mom, I could be a Nobel Prize Winner."

"Yes, I know you could." I responded.

My three daughters are accomplished. The oldest daughter, Suellen, is a business executive and international consultant. Her daughter is a sophomore in college and takes on campus leadership roles. Her son, a junior in high school plays percussion in the school band.

Daughter Audrey has put her math skills to work as an engineer and documents family growth through the lens of her camera. Her children are in 7th and 5th grades, strong in math and reading and active in Scouts.

Youngest daughter Emily has her own business or two businesses, one of home appraising, and the other of raising service dogs. The four grandchildren are evolving into fine people. The families read, travel, and have music in their lives.

My three daughters have survived horrific domestic abuse with stepfather/father, my second husband. All three daughters have partners who respect and love them.

Malcolm Gladwell discusses in his book, *Talking to Strangers*, his theory of "defaulting to truth" meaning, we interpret the world the way we want to see it or believe it to be. I think that I defaulted to truth when I believed that my second husband could do no wrong. My tenacity has been to believe in the positive as I see the world. I did not sense negative and thus did not raise my voice in protest. If there were clues of wrongdoing, or "red flags," I ignored them or did not believe they would apply in my case.

John Lewis has now given me the example of not letting up, to question what is wrong and be persistent in seeking justice. It is okay to get into "good trouble" by protesting injustice, Lewis said.

It took me five years from the time my oldest daughter revealed her stepfather's abuse to the Friday I was granted a divorce, and backed out of the driveway. Five years!

My hope in sharing this story is it will make a difference to someone who lives with an abuser, and that she or he will recognize their worth and beauty, grasp the courage to find their voice, and speak to abuse.

Barbara Young

Almost Thanksgiving
November 21, 2020

Dear Reader,

Fifty-three years have passed since I spoke with the elder in the interior of Brazil who gave me condolences for the death of Robert Kennedy. I felt a connection of international peace and love pass between us, and that moment remains memorable. Now, I sit at my computer, isolated as protection from COVID. Zelda, my black and white tabby cat, sleeps on her perch near my keyboard. In silence, she is present and gives me comfort. Zelda and I live alone and are preparing for Thanksgiving, A Thanksgiving to be spent not with family but just the two of us, caring for each other.

In this year of 2020, we have not had perfect vision, and we need to have a clearer insight for where we are going. While it is dark outside my window as I input my story, I feel the darkness, hatred and untruths that have soiled our politics. It has been a sad, difficult, and untrusting election season. Misinformation and disinformation remain, adding depth to the darkness.

Yet, I, too, believed when I took money to a bank account in New York I was doing so because my husband was serving his community in efforts to recycle equipment and dispose of toxic asbestos. I believed he was making the community a safer and cleaner place, doing work others would not do. I wonder now, years after my quick trips, how could I have been so gullible, so believing?

Barbara Young

Still Sheltered

December 2020

Dear Friend,

Sheltered in place and having the year 2020 to stay at home and explore my life, has been a gift. A gift because I have the time and space to reflect and to face the reality, the truth which I have been avoiding. I have been writing short stories for seven years, taking the prompts of writing teachers and recalling events of my childhood, a life shaped by events, places, and times. Through the months of 2020, alone with myself, I have found my voice. I have put fingers to the keyboard to touch truth. It is well past time to do so, but not too late. Having worn glasses since the seventh grade, I have used this year of 2020 to correct my vision.

I again hear the words of civil rights activist John Lewis when he advises us to "speak the truth, stand up for justice." In a recent week-long series on Childhood Trauma on the PBS NewsHour, experts spoke of the trauma endured by our children, and as parents and teachers, we must listen to their pain and help them recover with healthy, loving, and healing guidance. Politically, we must hear the pain of children and their parents separated from each other at our southern border. And those fleeing torture. We must hear their voices.

Barbara Young

Shocked, Dismayed, Saddened
January 7, 2021

My Fellow Americans,

I discussed domestic violence and childhood trauma in my last letter. Yesterday, I witnessed national violence and adult trauma, an all-of-us trauma. A large group of American citizens, long used to freedom of expression, stormed the United States Capitol to interfere with our democratic process in transfer of power. I sat in horror as I watched the news, picturing a white-faced mob carrying American flags and using the flags to shatter windows and doors and beat Capitol policemen. In their siege, they struck Officer Brian Sicknick, who died the next day, of injuries. Many protestors wrapped themselves in Trump flags; others carried flags of the Confederacy now considered outdated, inappropriate, and discriminatory, symbols of white supremacy. As the mob pushed forward to breach the halls of our country's 'Temple of Legislation,' they trampled

Rosanne Boyland allowing her to die at their feet. Tragic, too that Ashli Barritt, a US. Air Force veteran, embracing conspiracy theories was killed in the siege, attempting to enter the Speakers' Lobby through a smashed glass partition. Ashli fought in Iraq and came home to believe in the lies of her Commander-in-Chief, and following his order, joined the mob that stormed the Capitol. What happened to these people who called themselves "Patriots?" Do they know the Constitution and for what it stands? Have they forgotten what they learned in high school Civics? If they studied Civics at all. How could they have succumbed to false conspiracy theories? How could they not see that the President was lying to them? So many questions to ask.

I was quick to criticize those who attacked the Capitol. It was wrong, horrible, frightening. Yet, it has taken me years to reflect on my own behavior of not questioning what was going on within my own family. I failed to seek the truth and believed in the lies of second husband. Freddie and the former president led us to believe their untruths, their make believes. They both covered up bad behavior by projecting blame. Those at the Capitol insurrection and I in my marriage defaulted to the truth we thought to be true.

David Brooks, commenter on the PBS NewsHour January 8th said, "Our Citadel of Democracy has been desecrated." Webster defines the word desecrate as "treat (a sacred place or thing) with violent disrespect; violate." My daughters were desecrated, violated, by their stepfather. Our Capitol and our Constitution have been desecrated by the former President. Freddie McMurray was an alias when I met him, a lie from the beginning. Mr. Trump, the man who called himself President, was a lie when he said he would be our leader. The actions of these two men must not go unrecognized, unpublished, ignored, or brushed under the carpet. Bring them to justice.

Barbara Young

Wearing mask
Received COVID vaccine
February 2021

Dear Reader, my Friend,

With the peaceful transfer of leadership on January 20, 2021, I felt as though a great burden had been lifted from my shoulders. Within a few days, I was feeling less pain in my left hip and was walking more upright. Instead of being cloistered in my house, I took to the streets in my neighborhood and walked a loop of twenty blocks. The ceremony on the Capitol steps, the same steps violated by the January 6 insurrection, was filled with past presidents and leaders of Congress and the Supreme Court. I had tears when Lady Gaga sang the national anthem, Jennifer Lopez This Land Is Your Land," and Garth Brooks, Amazing Grace. It was Amanda Gorman's poem, The Hill We Climb, that spoke to my heart, filling me with hope. Amanda concluded her poem with these words:

For there is always light,
if only we're brave enough to see it
If only we're brave enough to be it."

The voices of these four performers reached into my heart, and I sat crying. Even as an older woman, sheltered-in-place in Olympia on Puget Sound, I, too, can raise my voice… ask the questions… speak to the truth… sit with those of different opinions and politics and find common ground that gives our beloved country purpose. Even as a simple girl from Dayton, Ohio, I can do my part. Hear my voice.

Barbara Young

71. Conclusion

THE SNOW IS FALLING IN OLYMPIA. I snuggle into the easy chair, wrap around me a handwoven wool throw, enjoy the quiet of the street, and relax seeing a blanket of white out my picture window. I smile thinking of family. My daughters are happy with their families and successful with their work. All three are positive, active parents, politically engaged, addressing injustice, and they are beautiful people. I have returned to playing the violin and piano, and I listen to the space between the notes. Beethoven said it was the most important, this space between the notes. We apply Beethoven's thinking to how we listen to each other. It is the pause between the stories that is the most important. We take time to listen and hear what the other is saying.

As the Native women taught me on the reservation—pass the talking stick, be still and listen, hear the stories of loss, love, and hope. And when COVID is no longer a spreader of illness and death, we will remove our facial covering and speak out. Please, hear my voice.

Barbara Young

Olympia, Washington,
December 28, 2021

73. Acknowledgements

I ACKNOWLEDGE MY PARENTS for my birth into a city that was to become the go-to place for swing politics. Born in 1942, Dayton was a hot spot and nerve center for inventors, industrialists, and a code-breaking center for the war effort.

For nine years, I have been writing short stories in response to prompts with writing instructors Keith Eisner, Anne Robinson, Jeff Birkenstein, Olivia Archibald, and Jim Lynch. Writing Group: Dan Jorgenson, Christine Colyar, Bonnie Cotton, Pat Bartley, Martha Worcester, Barbara Davis, and Jean Delastrata critiqued these chapters. Colleague Joyce Zerwekh critiqued. Doug Keck spent many hours on chapter layout and coaching me on the technology of putting a book together. Bob Cornelis added graphic art. Carolyn Keck checked grammar. Candace Palmo and Keith Eisner edited. Sharon Williams read and commented. Carolyn Rospierski was managing editor and project director. Ceramics professor Joe Batt taught me to work the clay, and welding professor John Goss taught me to be safe with the welding torch. Judith Altruda taught me to construct the mask and release the story. Women of the tribe taught me to weave. Poetry pen pal Frances Lee Heminway read, encouraged, commented. Barbara Packard gave me support to get the job done, read every page I brought to her, and pushed me to complete the work. Olivia read and helped with the final composition. Thank you all.

It is my daughters who inspired me to begin this writing and to stick to it. Their accomplishments I discussed in my letter September 1, 2020. Their courage, perseverance, belief in me and loving me despite my mistakes, their talents and their accomplishments helped me to complete this story. They raise questions and seek to make just the injustice in our society. My daughters, their friends, and my grandchildren are our hope for the future, maintaining the democracy in which questions are raised, and debate honored.

What became of Freddie McMurray you might ask? I acknowledge I was wife number three. I had lunch with wife four. Emily met wife five. I am not interested in keeping count.

Barbara Mould Young

About the Author

BARBARA MOULD YOUNG, MN, MHP, RN made a career in public health and teaching. She studied nursing at The Ohio State University, earned her Master of Health Planning at the University of Cincinnati and her Master of Nursing at University of Washington. She has taught at the University of Washington, Tacoma, St. Martin's University where she was Director of Nursing, West Seattle Community College, and South Puget Sound Community College.

In her first marriage, she served in the United States Peace Corps in Brazil. In her second marriage, she moved from Cincinnati to Richmond to Houston. When she divorced, she moved to Olympia, Washington. In 1995, she was called to a small Indian reservation on the Pacific Coast to be project director of a grant, "Return to Health: Reducing Sociocultural Barriers to Heath Care." The Native women taught her to weave cedar baskets and to make masks, and she began incorporating art and writing into her work. She has offered mask making workshops in cities across the country and at the University of Beijing. Mask making art morphed into ceramic and steel mediums. Barbara has three daughters, four grandchildren and lives Olympia, Washington.

Barbara's documentary video *Opening Doors: 100 Years of Public Health Nursing*, received the Creative Achievement Award, Public Health Nursing Section of the American Public Health Association, the Media Award from American Academy of Nursing, and the Bronze Apple Award from National Education Association. Her mask-making seminars have been presented at the American Public Health Association, the universities of Washington, St. Martin's, La Salle, the Nurse Training School, University of Beijing, as well as women's retreats and ArtsOlympia. La Salle University School of Nursing selected Barbara for the Year 2000 Distinguished Lecture. Barbara received commendation from Rosalyn Carter and Washington Governor Gary Locke for her work in immunizations. She swam for gold in the Washington State Senior Games, qualifying her to swim at the National Senior Games Association in Pittsburgh 2023.

This is a story of how a middle-American woman can overcome personal setbacks to spend a lifetime giving back into the community her skill, love, and attention. It illustrates a lesson Americans need more than ever at this moment in history.

Frances Lee Heminway, painter, potter, writer, poet, friend.

Hear My Voice is the perfect title for Barbara Mould Young's memoir. Her voice—as child, teenager, young woman, Peace Corps Volunteer, mother, wife, nurse, and mask maker—resonates through the many twists and turns of her story. Ultimately, *Hear My Voice* is a tale of becoming, of learning to hear and trust one's own voice—a highly relevant lesson for these times.

Keith Eisner, Writing Instructor, Olympia, Washington.
Author, *Blue Dot* published in The O. Henry Prize Stories, 2017.

Barbara Young's book *Hear My Voice: My Life Unmasked* brings new directions to the genre of the memoir. Rather than just relying on concise prose descriptions and inspirational insights, she underpins her stories through photos, images, and the occasional poetic line. Barbara's journey to discover meaning, purpose, and community through mask making becomes a story of grace, power, and awakening. The result is a beautifully crafted book full of hope and honesty.

Olivia Archibald, PhD.
Professor Emeritus of English.
Saint Martin's University.

CPSIA information can be obtained
at www.ICGtesting.com
Printed in the USA
LVHW051519220323
742294LV00020B/922